LIVING
WITH THE
END
IN MIND

LIVING
WITH THE
END
IN MIND

A PRACTICAL CHECKLIST FOR
LIVING LIFE TO THE FULLEST BY
EMBRACING YOUR MORTALITY

ERIN TIERNEY KRAMP
AND DOUGLAS H. KRAMP
WITH EMILY P. McKHANN

Three Rivers Press
New York

Published by Three Rivers Press, a division of Crown Publishers, Inc., 201 East 50th Street, New York, New York 10022. Member of the Crown Publishing Group.

Random House, Inc. New York, Toronto, London, Sydney, Auckland www.randomhouse.com

THREE RIVERS PRESS and colophon are trademarks of Crown Publishers, Inc.

Printed in the United States of America

Design by Rhea Braunstein

Library of Congress Cataloging-in-Publication Data

Kramp, Erin Tierney.
Living with the end in mind : a practical checklist for living life to the fullest by embracing your mortality / by Erin Tierney Kramp, Douglas H. Kramp, and Emily P. McKhann.
p.   cm.
Includes index.
1. Death—Handbooks, manuals, etc.   I. Kramp, Douglas H.
II. McKhann, Emily P.   III. Title.
BD444.K73   1998   98-27575
155.9'37—dc21   CIP

ISBN 0-609-80381-6

10 9 8 7 6 5 4 3 2 1

First Edition

For our parents
Thank you for your love, laughter and example

And, for Peyton
We love you infinity times infinity that never ends

CONTENTS

ACKNOWLEDGMENTS

Writing this book while fighting a terminal illness took the cumulative inspiration of many hearts and minds. In particular, we are forever indebted to our friend Emily McKhann, whose writing talents, keen mind, endless conference calls, numerous visits to Dallas, and boundless passion for life made this book a reality. Supporting the three of us each step of the way was her husband and our friend, Andy Cooper.

We are also thankful for the special people in our lives:

Our extraordinary daughter, Peyton, whose contagious smile, joyful laughter and loving soul have served as daily touchstones to what is pure and important in this world.

Erin's parents, Tom and Luanne Tierney, whose love and endless sacrifices have been some of the greatest blessings we have ever known. Like an eye of a hurricane, they have given us peace and comfort while the challenges of our lives have swirled around us. Having the time and energy to produce this book would have been impossible without their enduring support.

Doug's parents, Harley and Esther Kramp, who have inspired and enriched us by exemplifying timeless, basic values and spiritual depth throughout their lives.

Our respective families: Debbie and Jeff Webb and Nicholas and Tierney Branda; Noreen, John, Evan, and Tierney Simpson; Mike and Lisa Tierney; Jeff, Marcy, and Tanner Kramp; Marshall and Elsie Jarrett; the Erbachs; the Tierneys; and the Kramps.

Our dear friends Skip Hollingsworth and Geoffrey Marchant, whose thoughtful comments and edits on this book helped bring it all together.

Our agent, Neeti Madan, and our editor, Kristin Kiser, who have supported us and this book with unwavering enthusiasm and a willingness to go the extra mile.

We have been blessed to have friends whose unconditional love, countless prayers, and timely assistance have given us joy, comfort, and most important, spiritual and physical strength. In particular, we would like to thank the following people for contributing in their own way to the content of this book:

Lori Abernathy, the Andersons, Barbara Anderson, Carl Anderson, Wayne Atwood, Patty Aubrey, Kathy Austin, Grace Avery, the Baileys, the Bairds, Julianna Baise, Katz Baker, Katzy Barker, the Barneses, Erin Barrington, Bill Bagley, Mary Bass, the Beckwiths, the Beletics, Don Benton and his family, the Bernhardts, the Berrys, Dr. Blumenschein, the *incredible* team and patients at the Arlington Cancer Center and the *awesome* nurses at Arlington Infusion Center and on the third floor of the Arlington Memorial Hospital, the Boeckmans, Trigg Bracewell, Nancy Brinker, Bob Brown, the Browns, David Bruce, James Brychta, the Buckenhams, the Campbells, Shari Campbell, Jack Canfield, the Caraways, Cathy Carolla, the Carters, Lylene Cecil, the Chapmans, E. Clark, Jackie Coberly, Jo Coke, the Colemans, the Collins, the Conners, contributors to the Erin Tierney Kramp Encouragement Award, the Cooks, Esther Cooper, the supportive team at Corporate Communications Center, Stephen Covey, the Coxes, Rev. Mark Craig, the Creixells, the Cutlers, the Darvers, Mary Davis, Tracy Day, Ernie Deal, the Deckers, the Dedmans, the DeRuffs, Dr. Karel Dicke, Marilyn Dickson, Hugh Downs, the Duncans, the Duprees, the Dyers, Jackie Ebenholtz, Tommi Elliott, the Enholms, the Ericksons, Lisa Erspamer, Paul Ervin, Elizabeth Esperson, Joel Fleishman, the Flints, Focus on the Family, Trisha Fusch, Karen Gaabucayan, the Gallivans, Angel Garcia, the Garners and their great team at A+ student staffing, the

Gaylords, the Garvins, the Glens, the Goldbergs, the Gold-steins, the Goyanises, Father Graham, the Grogans, the Grozas, Marcus Guardiola, Janice Guthrie, the Halls, the Hammonds, the Hamners, the Harelsons, the Harphams, Tom Harrison, the Harts, Dorothy Henderson, Kathryn Henkel, Kim Hibbs, French Hill, the Hillers, the Hockaday and St. Marks Classes of 1980 and 2010, John Holzgraeffe, David Hook, Fran Hopkins, Regen Horchow, Kathleen Howard, the Huffines, the Huseltons, the Hutchinsons, Lee A. Iacocca, Carol Irwin, Susan Istre, the Jeffersons, Sara Johnston, the Karsotises, Frank Kehr, the Kennedys, the Keelers, the Klines, the Knapps, Bob Kohler, Hamid Kooros, the Kormans, Sharon Kraus, the Krauses, Suzi Kriscunas, Lisa LaMaster, Mr. and Mrs. Tom Landry, Tom Landry Jr., Larry Lang, Susanna Langs, the Laws, Lou Lebowitz, Elizabeth Lee, the Leuschels, the Leyendeckers, Cheryl Lilley, the Lindsleys, Joy Lindsey, the Loewinsohns, the Lonemans, Joe Longino, the Louises, the Lynches, the Mackenzies, the Maclays, Liz Makely, Earline Maloy, Lisa Margolis, Stephen Marrow, the Marshalls, the Martins, the Masatoses, Jay McAuley, the McGraws, the McKhanns, Guy McKhann and Marilyn Albert, Fran McKinley, the McManemins, the McNamaras, the Meaders, the Meeks, the Meiers, the Moirs, Nancy Moon, Greg Morgan, Susan Morgan, the Mosleys, Cooper Munroe, the Murchisons, the Murdochs, Don Nauly, Ann O'Neal, the Nelsons, Olivia Newton-John, Rex Nichols, Pete and Riley Norman, Taffie Norris, the Northrups, the nurses at Olsten, the O'Donnells, the O'Sullivans, the Oziers, the wonderful people at PageMart, Sally Paine, the Pardues, Laura Pendergrass, the Perots, Licia Petmecky, the Phillipsons, the Pickens, Connie Pittman, the Powells, Carol Powers, Sharon Quist, the Rafkins, Traver Rains, the Ratelles, Dr. Joshua Rettig, Carron Richardson, Teri Rife, Ene Riisna, the Ronchettis, Gail Rola, Frances Rowland, Dr. Alan Rubin, the Rundells, the Rutherfords, the Sachs, the Scotts, the Seidels, the Shelmires, Helen Shift, Angel Shook, the Shums, Dee Silverstein, the Slaughters, Wes Small, Rev. Bill

Smith, the Soderquists, Robin Soloman, Lisa Sparkman, Lori Sparks, the Stanleys, Aryn Stapp, Amy Rhodes Stephenson, Jack Stone Jr., Becky Story, the Stiebers, Bronson Stocker, Don Stroddel, the Tangs, Cindy Tarrant, Catherine Tuck, Brad Urschel #10, the Urschels, the Vaughns, Danny Walker and his family, Cindy Walkup, the Wallaces, Barbara Walters, the Waltons, the Weinkaufs, Johnny Pate and Pat Weir, Anne Marie Weiss, the Weisses, Bob Whitman, Trisha Wilson, Will Taylor, Terry Winborn, Oprah Winfrey and her outstanding staff, and the Woodalls.

And most important, we give thanks to our Lord, who made this beautiful trip possible.

LIVING
WITH THE
END
IN MIND

INTRODUCTION

❧

I once thought if I knew I had only a year to live, I would travel around the world for the entire time. I would live a life that was full of adventure until my last dying day. In actuality, that's not what I chose to do. When I realized my time might be short, I immediately wanted to spend as much of it as possible with the people I cared for most, doing things together that we enjoyed or believed in. The way I saw it, my family, friends, and I had too much to share and too many things to say to one another for me to go gallivanting off. This was an enormous shift for me. If my family and friends were the most important aspect of my life, why was I spending so little time with them? Why were we letting superficial conversations pass for intimacy when there were so many more important things to talk about together? Once I started down that path, I started looking at all my priorities in life. Acknowledging my own mortality and preparing for my eventual death changed my whole focus. Since that time, more than four years ago, I have certainly had some great adventures, but they have occurred within a context of knowing my priorities and what makes me feel happy and at peace.

This checklist started out as a letter I wrote to two friends before they passed away. They were not at all prepared for their deaths—no wills, no funeral arrangements, no caregivers for their children. They were in denial until their last moments. I had pleaded with both of them a few weeks before their respective deaths that, as responsible adults, they and their healthy spouses should do some preparation, in the event that any one of them passed away suddenly. But it was too late for both of them. The panic had set in, and they were immobilized. Both were utterly frightened and superstitious that preparing to die would imply they had given up hope and thus would hasten their deaths.

My husband, Doug, and I found the complete opposite to be true. When we created this checklist to prepare for our eventual deaths, we felt enormously relieved to have taken care of many of the little "what ifs" associated with the possibility of dying. Our stress decreased significantly, and the most incredible transformation occurred. We started living life moment by moment with a complete sense of where we were headed, what we wanted the end of our lives to look like when we sat down with God, how we wanted to treat each other, what we individually wanted out of our lives, and even how we wanted to parent.

When we shared early drafts of the checklist with our family members and friends, the response was overwhelming. People repeatedly told us they saw their lives shift in profound and powerful ways after working on their checklists. They said they discovered a heightened sense of themselves and their unique purpose in life by facing up to death and living with the end in mind. We started to hear from friends of friends who wanted to receive copies of the checklist. We heard from healthy people who were interested in what we had learned and wanted to apply the lessons to their own lives. Many letters came from people whose parents had died when they were young. These letter writers were particularly moved by the checklist and wished their parents had thought to leave them special remembrances before they died. We also heard from people who were sick or who, for one reason or another, were contemplating their mortality. Finally, we received calls from the caregivers, families, and friends of people who were ill.

Then, our minister mentioned our work to a writer for *The Dallas Morning News*, who wrote a feature story on us. After seeing the newspaper article, an internationally syndicated radio show interviewed us and printed thirty thousand copies of our early checklist. Emily McKhann, our friend and coauthor of this book, edited the original checklist and, while doing so, mentioned the concept to a friend in New York, who in turn notified *20/20*, which broadcast a story on us. The *20/20* producer, Ene Riisna, encouraged us to expand the pamphlet into a full-fledged book written for people who are healthy. Shortly thereafter, Oprah Winfrey invited us to appear on her show to discuss the book. Oprah followed that show with another show that featured her favorite noncelebrity guests since 1986—and we were among them!

It has been an incredible string of events, not the least of which has been seeing this checklist touch a chord in people. More than ever, we are finding that people are interested in thinking and talking about issues associated with their mortality. The mountains of letters and E-mail messages we have received seem to share a common theme—that people want to live their lives more fully by accepting and embracing the eventuality of death.

We hope you will find this checklist to be a useful tool for *living* your life to its fullest.

GUIDELINES FOR USING THIS CHECKLIST

To get the most out of this checklist, we suggest following several guidelines:

1. Take your time. Use this checklist to get closer to the people you love and to find a renewed sense of purpose. The last thing we want is for your life to become focused solely on preparing to die. We recommend reading the book through before deciding which checklist items to work on first. Then, you can start working on the chapter that interests you most, a little at a time.

2. Share the checklist with someone you love, if possible. Doug and I got as much out of discussing the checklist items and issues as we did completing them. In the process, we learned about ourselves, each other, and our relationship. We also found it helpful to take responsibility for different items on the list once we had agreed on our approach. That way, we could get the checklist done more quickly and share with each other the insights we learned along the way.

3. If you are living with illness, choose the items on the checklist that will give you peace with your eventual death. Only you know what those are. We had years to create this checklist, while you might have less time. Know that whatever preparations you complete in advance of your death are a gift to yourself and your loved ones.

4. Feel free to invent your own checklist items. We designed the checklist to stimulate your thinking. It is not all-inclusive. You probably will think of new checklist items to complete as you go about your own preparations and define your own priorities.

1

Why Embrace Mortality When the Ultimate Goal Is to Live?

*We have come to believe that by embracing your mortality
—whether you are in perfect health or are ill—
you can live a more purposeful, peaceful, and joyful life.*

Why should you read a book about embracing your mortality when the ultimate goal is to live? The answer to that question is exactly the reason Doug and I wrote this checklist. Because death informs life. We can go about our day-to-day lives, or we can use the knowledge that we all will die to gain perspective on what is important today—whether we are healthy or ill. When Doug and I faced up to our mortality, we were amazed by the positive changes that then occurred in our lives.

When doctors told us that I had "three to eighteen months to live," Doug and I were stunned. We still had so much to do together, so many things to say, so much planning to do for our daughter Peyton's future. I wasn't ready to think of Doug, Peyton, and my parents having to fend for themselves or sift through my unorganized life. I wasn't prepared to die.

None of us were. In textbook fashion, when we heard the grave news, we went into denial. We thought we could beat the disease, if only we had the right doctors and right treatments.

Then, as time went by, we couldn't ignore reality. Our unspoken worries and fears would not go away. After getting over the shock of my diagnosis, I needed to prepare myself, my family, and friends for the possibility of my death. It was time to get my life in order and to make things as easy as possible for my loved ones. Besides, I belatedly realized, we all will die eventually, either suddenly or slowly over time. I was the one diagnosed with a terminal disease, but Doug could be hit by a car and die tomorrow. We had no guarantees in life. It then occurred to me that knowing my estimated life expectancy was a gift, and it was up to me to make the most of this gift.

I was surprised by what happened when I accepted that I might die. Acknowledging death didn't become a morbid undertaking, as I had expected. Instead, it became an opportunity to discover a renewed sense of purpose in my life, get closer to my family and friends, and deepen my spirituality. For the first time, I actually set out to create balance in my life. My priorities clearly fell into place, and allocating my time became easy. I found myself becoming happier and more relaxed and began living a healthier life that, I believed, could very well extend my life expectancy. I actually attained a sense of my own *well-being*.

For most people, death and dying remain taboo topics. People routinely discuss subjects that were once considered off-limits, i.e., drugs, sex, religion, politics. Yet they feel uncomfortable talking about the prospect of their own death. Our most certain commonality as people—that we will all die—goes unexamined. Why is it that people plan their vacations, finances, weddings, and retirements, but do so little to plan for their deaths? My experience has been that acknowledging and preparing for one's death can give clarity of purpose. Living with the end in mind is not a gloomy thought, but rather a life-affirming opportunity to find peace and happiness.

By way of background, four years ago, I was a venture capitalist, and Doug was starting a new business unit in a large corporation. We had a happy marriage, a precious one-year-old daughter, a close extended family, good friends, and fulfilling careers. Then, shortly before I turned thirty-two, when I thought I was at the peak of health, we discovered I had cancer. Both Doug and I dealt with the disease much as we would approach a problem in business—researching all the angles, examining the options, bringing in the best team, and putting all our energies into finding a solution. For a year following the diagnosis, I continued to work while undergoing chemo treatments. I threw my energies into my career, all the while qualifying doctors, researching treatment options, and trying to keep my mind off the ramifications of the cancer's spreading.

For most of my adult life, I derived a pivotal part of my identity from my career. I liked the successes and the accolades that went with doing good work. Business felt like a high-stakes game, one that I knew well and thrived on playing. How my business colleagues perceived me was very important to my self-esteem. Stepping off the fast track would have been a great leap into the unknown that would have forced me to evaluate and redefine who I was as a person.

At the same time, though, in the back of my mind and in conversations with my husband, I struggled with questions regarding my spiritual beliefs and my purpose in life. I questioned whether I belonged on a different path. The thoughts nagged at me, but invariably I got caught up in my life and did not give myself the breathing room to explore these dimensions of myself.

Then we got the news that the cancer had spread to my spine. This meant that my chances of surviving had decreased enormously. Suddenly, life seemed short. The recurrence was the shock I needed to find the courage to stop working. I walked away from venture capital and took on the full-time job of looking after my physical, emotional, mental, and spiritual well-being.

The aggressive treatments were going well until about a year into the regimen, when I contracted an infection in my abdomen, caused by the high dose of chemotherapy. At the time, my white blood cell count was at zero, so my body could not fight the infection. My life was in terrible danger. The doctor told Doug and my parents that my odds of surviving the infection were minimal at best. I was placed in a sterile "bubble room" at the hospital and given massive doses of antibiotics. I was there for three weeks, barely conscious, while my husband and parents stayed continuously by my side, hoping and praying I would not die. On Easter morning, my white counts began to rise. No one could believe it. It was a miracle.

The bubble room experience had a profound effect on Doug and me. Doug told me afterwards he had panicked at the thought of my death. Until then, the reality of my situation had still not hit home. Yes, we had talked about my possibly dying, but he had not believed it could actually happen. Spending three weeks in the hospital, hoping and praying for my survival, tapped a whole new level of emotions for him. During those long fretful days, an endless stream of questions ran through his mind. He tried to recall my favorite color, season of the year, vacation, food, and music. These might have seemed trivial thoughts when I was doing fine, but Doug imagined our daughter, Peyton, asking these questions about her deceased mother. The thought of raising Peyton by himself penetrated his mental armor for the first time. Doug did not have the answers, and he did not know how he was going to manage without me.

When I left the bubble room, we learned the cancer had left my spine. Again, we had been given more time together—time to enjoy our lives together and prepare for the possibility that Doug and I might die before we were ready. We had learned our lesson: We would no longer go unprepared for the eventuality of our deaths. Neither one of us wanted to relive the panic we had felt when I almost died. With my near-death experience as a backdrop, we started talking together about our purpose in life, our most important priorities, the impact we each wanted to have on the world, our spiritual beliefs, and their relevance to our day-to-day lives. We talked and talked and took notes about our feelings and observations. Rather than getting dragged down by feelings of sadness or depression, as one might expect when contemplating death, we became energized and excited by these life-affirming and thought-provoking conversations. We had so much to learn about ourselves and about the emotional, physical, mental, and spiritual aspects of preparing for the possibility of dying.

As we addressed each point that came to mind and began creating this checklist, we felt calmer and more at peace with our lives. Answering tough questions for ourselves, defining our priorities, learning to communicate with each other, and making changes to our lives were huge, positive releases. We started to create a legacy for our family should either one of us pass away unexpectedly; it contained photo albums, letters, videos, and keepsakes. And we made the practical plans associated with our funerals, our estates, and end-of-life health care. We talked about our fears about death and our hopes and dreams for the future. With the checklist complete, we saw our lives come into focus, and we felt grounded. When we later learned that my cancer had again spread to other parts of my body, we felt more equipped to handle it. Whereas in the past the news would have thrown our world into a spin, we now felt we could manage almost anything that came at us.

As we were working on the checklist, Doug's mother became seriously ill. In the days leading up to her death, Doug, his brother, and father had to make major decisions on her medical treatment. Then, within forty-eight hours of her passing, they had to guess her preference for a coffin, the epitaph for her tombstone, her burial clothes, the prayers to be said and songs to be sung at the memorial service, and the person to give her eulogy. They also wrote the obituary, chose a photo to be displayed at the service, designated charities to receive gifts in lieu of flowers, and tracked down the phone numbers and addresses of friends and family members to inform them of Doug's mother's death.

At one of the most difficult and painful times in his life, Doug found himself swamped with responsibilities and difficult decisions. Doug returned to work after being away from the office for two weeks—one week by his mother's bedside, and another week planning and attending her funeral, taking care of her

estate, and helping his father organize her remaining belong-
ings. When he arrived back at the office, his coworkers assumed
he had had time to grieve, when in truth he had just been
through the most emotionally draining two weeks of his life.
Doug was exhausted to his core and had had no time to grieve
for his mother. If Doug's mother had had a chance to prepare
for the practical aspects of her death, her surviving family could
have spent more time comforting and being with one another,
instead of facing the mountain of details that needed immediate
attention after her death. The death of Doug's mother reinforced for us that the checklist could be a powerful tool for ourselves and for others. We came to believe that one of the most
loving and thoughtful gifts a person can give oneself and loved
ones is to be prepared.

Given all that we have learned, Doug and I would not trade
these years for anything. Without the struggle of the last years
and the threat of imminent death, we would have neither realized that accepting our mortality would shift our perspective in
such positive ways, nor seen that we were living with a false
sense of security. By looking at our priorities and purpose with
"the end in mind," our lives changed dramatically. We wish
everyone could get the perspective of having a life-threatening
disease without having to suffer from the disease itself.

This book is organized according to what we believe are the
four dimensions of all humans: the emotional, the physical, the
mental, and the spiritual. Taken together, these four dimensions
create a "whole person."

As an adult and before getting cancer, I relied almost solely on
my mind, or the mental dimension, in my day-to-day life. In
business, this was especially true. The more logical I was, the
more effective I became. If I let myself become emotional or
showed too much of my spiritual side, I believed others in business would discount my ideas and take me less seriously. Using
my mind became my "tool for success" and also my coping mechanism. My logical, reasoning side took over whether I was eval-

uating new business deals, organizing our family life, or deciding on cancer treatment options. My modus operandi was based on the belief that I could think through just about any problem and come up with a probable solution.

When I stopped working, I gave myself more leeway to examine and express my emotions and let my spiritual side have a say. I had not given myself such freedom since I was a child. What a revelation it was to find that these sides could coexist and balance each other! I enjoyed tapping into these other sides of myself and getting new insight into myself and the world around me. Up until then, intellectualizing had taken me only so far. Exploring my emotions and delving into my spiritual beliefs touched deeper chords. As I became more comfortable with each of these dimensions of myself, it became clear the checklist needed to be organized accordingly.

In creating this checklist, we defined the emotional, physical, mental, and spiritual dimensions as follows:

• **The Emotional.** I have always tended to look at emotions in terms of my feelings for myself, family members, and friends, my emotional maturity and stability and that of people around me, and what I had read about psychiatry, psychology, and theories on emotional well-being. When I considered the possibility of my death, however, very specific emotional concerns came into focus. How would I address my fear of death? What issues did I need to clear up with the people in my life, and what emotional legacies did I want to leave for those closest to me? How would I deal with my own emotions and help ease the grieving process for my family members and friends? Doug wondered how he would get by if he lost his wife and best friend. How would he parent our daughter without me? And how would he manage his own grief while doing his best to support our daughter through her grieving process? These questions and others became the framework for chapters 3 and 4.

• **The Physical.** Like many people, throughout my life, I have spent a considerable amount of time and energy trying to eat well and stay healthy, working out, choosing attractive clothes to wear, and being conscious of my waist size, hair style, and skin tone. When I thought about my body in terms of my eventual death, however, my orientation changed dramatically. I saw my physical body as the shell that housed my mind and spirit. When I died, that shell would need to be taken care of. Preparing for the physical aspects of my death included choosing burial or cremation, making burial arrangements, and deciding who would write the eulogy.

This chapter on preparing the body might be difficult for some people, so we have two suggestions. First, we've written this book so you can skip around. You can start wherever you feel most comfortable. If you want to go to another chapter and come back to this one when you feel ready, that's okay. Second, please don't skip it entirely. Our fears and superstitions tend to get the better of us, and once you start into this chapter, we're sure you will find it worthwhile. When you're finished, you as well as your loved ones will get the enormous sense of relief that comes with knowing your plans are in place.

• **The Mental.** How I think, how I process information, and my creativity make up the mental dimension. In light of that, when I looked at the inevitability of my death, I realized Doug and I faced an intellectual challenge in thinking through the details of our family's life—the organization of our household, estate planning, and finances. Handling these details required a cognitive ability, a processing of information that was different from any other mindset. In Chapter 6, we "put on our thinking caps" to organize essential paperwork and household functions.

• **The Spiritual.** I seem always to have been interested in spiritual issues. At different points in my life, I have studied the world's religions and, even just last year, worked with The Dallas Kindness Foundation to assist in publishing a booklet that highlighted the commonalities of fourteen religions (among them, Buddhism, Christianity, Hinduism, Islam, and Judaism). While I found these inquiries absorbing, I thought about my spiritual beliefs only sporadically and otherwise went about my busy life.

When I nearly died in the bubble room, spirituality took on a whole new importance for me. Suddenly I was able to define my beliefs, pray, reflect on my purpose in the world, and feel a loving connection to a higher being. I realized, as did Doug, that only through my spiritual side would I find peace with my eventual death. I came to believe that only my spirit will live on after I die—that my emotional, physical, and mental dimensions will all die with me. Regardless of wealth, social status, physical prowess, or mental abilities, my internal joy at the point of death would rest solely on my spiritual well-being. Thus, integrating my spiritual side into the other dimensions of my life has become central to achieving balance and happiness for me. Chapter 7 looks at defining one's spiritual beliefs in the context of one's eventual death.

In the next chapter of this book, we recommend creating a legacy for your loved ones—mementos and remembrances that they can treasure for years to come after you pass away. Since legacies are personal keepsakes of your life and can encompass all dimensions of your personality—the emotional, the physical, the mental, and the spiritual—chapter 2 includes all four dimensions, as does chapter 8, the final chapter in the book, "Expect to Live," which looks at living with the end in mind and at ways of living life fully, surrounded by love and laughter.

2

LEAVING A LEGACY FOR THE PEOPLE YOU LOVE

❦

What do legacies have to do with embracing your mortality? Since working on this book, I have heard from innumerable people whose loved ones had previously died very suddenly. After they recovered from the terrible shock of the death, many people anguished over not having more by which to remember their father or mother, partner, child or friend.

Doug and I think it is important to leave a legacy for the people we especially love; for us, that means for each other, our daughter, our parents, and friends. While the most important legacies are our memories of happy times shared together, we have found that tangible things such as letters, scrapbooks, photographs and albums, audiotapes, videotapes, and mementos can reinforce these happy recollections. For example, after Doug, Peyton, and I look through photo albums of family trips or gatherings, we tend to remember those occasions more vividly than we would otherwise. Rereading a letter Doug wrote to me years ago reminds me of conversations and feelings from years past.

A friend shared with me another letter shortly after my cancer diagnosis. This letter, which had a tremendous impact on my life, read:

Dear Maggie:

I bought this book, Mom Remembers: A Treasury of Memories for My Child, *for myself to use, but I would like to give it to Erin to use for Peyton. My mother died when I was very young and I am realizing that I miss my mom the older I get. So, encourage Erin to leave memories for Peyton when she is older. Maybe her father, a relative, or a friend could give her things as she is ready for them. This book is a great and fun way to pass along information. Oh, how I wish I had this filled out by my mom. Other things I wanted to know include:*

1) *What each age was like for her (elementary school, junior high, high school).*
   - *Her favorite subjects and teachers*
   - *Her friends and boyfriends*
   - *Hobbies*
   - *Dreams (what she aspired to be and do)*
   - *Mistakes and advice for that age.*

   It would be fun to have a mini-time capsule for each age. For example, sample papers, report cards, pictures and stories from that point in her life.
2) *A video of my mom talking to me. Maybe words of advice and what she admires about me. Also, challenges in life I may face. A video of her and me together would be great—just to see how we interacted.*
3) *I would love to know all about her engagement and wedding. For example, how she picked out her dress, flowers, bridesmaids, etc. Plus, maybe honeymoon tips and suggestions.*
4) *I want to know about her marriage—why she fell in love with my father and how their dating relationship was. Also, what qualities did she look for in a partner? Plus:*
   - *Tips on marriage: Why she loved being married to my father.*
   - *Her favorite recipes or favorite things to do.*

- *Traditions she started*
  (Because, after her death, we no longer had any).

5) *Motherhood—The joys and hard times she felt about raising me.*

6) *How much she loves me. I would also like a letter reminding me to trust the Lord. I would love to hear about her relationship with God and what He taught her through her illness.*

7) *I really wish I would have had a letter that could be read each birthday or Christmas (even the same letter) to make my mother seem like part of the holiday.*

8) *I also wish I had a letter from her on my wedding day—That was the hardest part of my life without a mom!*

9) *A picture of just her and me together—framed with a note ("I love you")—would be a much treasured item for me.*

I really want Erin to know that Peyton will always remember her. Each year I long for my mother even more and Erin can fill so many gaps in Peyton's life by leaving her these things.

Signed,
Lori Abernathy

Lori's letter was powerful. It inspired me to express my love for Peyton in so many different ways. For Doug and Peyton, I wanted to create legacies that they could treasure in years to come and might even want to share with future generations. Both Doug and I realized that creating this legacy for my family was one of the most important aspects our preparations for my possible death from this disease.

➤ Even if you are strong and healthy, by creating legacies, you can give your loved ones gifts that they can treasure for years and generations to come.

➤ The two most important aspects of creating an emotional legacy are for you (1) to convey your love for your family and friends, and (2) to enjoy the process. We also recommend creating legacies that let you share what is unique about you. We received countless letters from people who lost their parents, friends, or partners. What they most wanted to know about these people was what made them special.

➤ Before you dive into the chapter, a word of caution. I recommend allocating as little or as much time to this process as you feel comfortable with. While creating a legacy might make you feel emotional, it should never feel like a chore. Doug and I worked on the items on the checklist when we felt like it. We enjoyed thinking and talking about each new project and had a lot of fun working together. In addition, we learned a great deal about ourselves and, by thinking ahead, came up with new ways of parenting Peyton day to day.

➤ Let me add that we had years to work on this. Please don't feel overwhelmed by the size of this checklist. Choose the items that excite you and do those. If, after time, other items on the checklist capture your imagination, do them as well. Enjoy!

❏ **Organize and place your photographs in albums, and record audiotapes to be played while looking through the albums.**

Over the years, we accumulated a huge number of photographs that had never been organized. Like many of our friends, we tucked our pictures and negatives into shoe boxes, drawers, and closets throughout the house. Trying to find a particular picture was like trying to find an ant in a pepper shaker (except at least an ant would move!).

For my thirtieth birthday, Doug assembled an album of photographs taken of me throughout my life. The album had more than two hundred pictures and took him three months to complete, working during evenings and occasional weekends. It was a great birthday surprise and a real treasure. After my cancer diagnosis a few years later, Doug decided to organize all our photographs and negatives. It was a sizable undertaking, to say the least, but he had four strong reasons to get it done: (1) If I died soon, the picture albums would be an invaluable remembrance of our lives together. (2) Looking at the albums with Peyton would reinforce her early memories of her mother. (3) He probably would not have the emotional resources to complete the task if I died now. Besides, if I lived, we would enjoy the albums for years to come.

Thus began the "Photo Marathon Project." Whenever he could find a bit of time, Doug worked on the photo albums. He sat in the room where I was resting so we could look at the photos together and relive our fond memories. When he completed each album, Doug, Peyton, and I tape-recorded our recollections as we flipped through the pages. We put the finished tapes in a sleeve, which we had glued to the inside cover. What started out as a daunting project became a labor of love that gave us a great chance to spend time together and reminisce.

While Doug was putting together our pictorial history, I enlisted the help of my parents and a local video store to catalogue and organize our family videotapes. We duplicated our videos on archive-quality tape (ordinary videotape breaks down over time) and labeled each tape with detailed information on its contents. For Doug's thirty-sixth birthday, my parents and I presented him with a complete set of our videotapes organized in chronological order.

By organizing both the photographs and videotapes, we put "lost" family treasures at our fingertips. Our friends have loved looking at the albums and finding pictures of themselves sharing good times with us. I have found Peyton alone several times, flipping through the pages of an album, and have wondered what was going through her head as she looked at her infant pictures with Mommy, Daddy, and grandparents taking turns holding her. Doug and I have often said, if our house ever caught fire, we would make sure our family members were safe, and then we would grab our photo albums and home video library. To ensure the safety of some of our most valuable negatives and videos, we intend to store them in a fireproof safe.

Consistent with other checklist items, working on the photo albums gave Doug some unexpected benefits. Reliving the fond memories took Doug's mind off his day-to-day challenges. He felt refreshed and uplifted by the project and was reminded of the blessings in our lives. And now we have a legacy to enjoy for the rest of our lives.

❏ **Write letters to your loved ones telling them how much they mean to you.**

It is so easy to go through life assuming our friends and family members know how much they mean to us, when in truth there is nothing quite so eye-opening and uplifting as articulating why we find the people in our life incredible. Doug wrote his mother and father letters on their seventieth birthdays, telling them how much they meant to him. In the letters, he wrote several paragraphs on each stage of his life: childhood, teenage years, and adulthood. Doug described in detail what he had learned from them and acknowledged the contributions and the sacrifices they had made for him. They already knew he loved them, but these letters articulated the many ways in which their presence in his life had shaped and influenced him. Both his mother and father treasured their letters, saying they were the greatest gifts he had ever given them. (As a side note, when Doug's mother died at the age of seventy-three, Doug referred back to her seventieth birthday letter when he wrote her eulogy.)

❏ **Keep a journal that might be shared with others in case you pass away.**

Since learning I had cancer, I have kept a journal in which I have written my thoughts, described activities and enjoyable moments, quoted favorite poems and scripture, attached interesting clippings, and (on occasion) doodled. I have planned for this journal to go to Peyton after I die, so I have given special attention to writing about the times we have shared together and her magical traits as a little girl. The journal stays by my bedside so I can pick it up at a moment's notice and write even just a few words. Sometimes, I write more lengthy pieces about what's on my mind, and other times I remark on what I find beautiful about the people who surround me. There is no set format, just the thought that my daughter will have one more way to get to know me should I pass away before she grows up.

Over the years, Doug too has kept a diary in which he tracked the highlights of our lives. In particular he has documented Peyton's numerous "firsts."

➤ Journals can be written for anyone you care for deeply. Some people might prefer to write a journal for themselves, without having to worry about who might read it later. Then, when the volume is well under way, you can decide if someone should receive the journal in the event of your death.

❏ **Fill out a "Remember Book."**

A "Remember Book" is a type of diary in which a person can write his or her recollections of life. With blank pages that have different headings at the top, Remember Books are designed to stimulate the writer's memory. Pages might have such headings as: My Earliest Memories, Most Memorable Teachers, Favorite Summer Activities, My First Car, Important Life Lessons, Favorite Leisure Time Activities, Most Awe-Inspiring Books or Movies. Remember Books can be filled out for anyone in your life—parents, spouse, trusted companion, children, best friend.

Remember Books come in all shapes and sizes. Following are the titles of several I have come across:

- *The Book of Myself: A Do-It-Yourself Autobiography in 201 Questions,* by Carl and David Marshall
- *Journal to the Soul,* by Rose Offner
- *To My Daughter, With Love,* by Donna Green

Working on my Remember Book, I had a lovely time reminiscing about my life and thinking of tidbits that Peyton, Doug, and my parents might find funny or interesting later in life.

❏ **Designate any items, such as jewelry, to be given to family members or friends on special occasions.**

I arranged for my daughter to receive pieces of my jewelry when she reaches important points in her life, such as her eighth grade, high school and college graduations, sixteenth, eighteenth and twenty-first birthdays, and her wedding day. To each piece, I attached handwritten notes that included words of wisdom for each point in her life.

I also took Peyton to a jewelry store, and we picked out different charms that reminded us of activities we shared together. For example, we picked out a snowflake that reminded us of the time it snowed late one night after Peyton went to bed. Where we live in Texas, it rarely snows. I convinced my husband, who is from the snowy state of Ohio, to wake Peyton so she could enjoy the snow before it melted in the early morning. We put on mittens and hats and all stuck our tongues out to catch snowflakes. All three of us will never forget it. She is to receive a charm every Christmas, beginning with the Guardian Angel charm. I wrote a letter with each charm, talking about the memory that the charm represented and my love for her. (I purchased the charms from a prominent national jewelry chain. In the event she loses the bracelet, it can be replaced easily. In my letters, I explained to Peyton that the importance of the charms is their meaning, not the actual charms themselves.)

❏ **Designate personal mementos or heirlooms to be given to family members or friends upon your death.**

Too often people die, leaving their family members to squabble over who gets what of the estate. Dividing up an estate can be a heart-wrenching experience, particularly if there are numerous heirs involved. We think it is much nicer is to set aside favorite mementos and heirlooms for people individually. That way, if things are divided equally with consideration for each heir's wishes and interests, the heirs can feel as though they received special gifts that were meant especially for them. For example, Doug's grandmother noted in her will that Doug should receive a baby rocker that he loved as a child. The rocker had been given to his grandmother by her father on her first birthday. On that day, a horse-drawn furniture wagon pulled up to their farmhouse. The furniture salesman hopped down off the wagon and told Doug's great-grandfather about some of the furniture he had to sell. When he showed him the baby rocker, Doug's great-grandfather bought it on the spot for his one-year-old daughter. Knowing the story behind the rocker—and knowing that Doug's grandmother specifically designated the rocker for him—make it an invaluable treasure.

My coauthor, Emily, received an antique silver fork after her grandfather died. The fork had an initial "E" engraved on it (her grandmother's name was Elizabeth) and came in a flannel sack to protect it from tarnishing. On the outside of the sack, her grandfather had pinned a small piece of paper on which he had written "Emily" in his neat, elegant handwriting. To this day, Emily treasures the small fork, tucked in its little bag with the piece of paper still pinned to the outside.

There are many ways to leave mementos for loved ones. Should I die from this disease, I have instructed Doug to take material from many of my clothes and have a love quilt made out of it for Peyton. Here are some other ideas for mementos or heirlooms.

FAVORITE BOOKS	Write an inscription saying why you love the book and why you want the person to have it.
CHILDREN'S BOOKS	1. Give to your children the books that they loved when they were young. Inscribe when and where

the books were read, how much the child liked them, and what the child used to say about each book. 2. Give the books you most loved as a child to someone who might appreciate them. Add inscriptions.

KORAN, BIBLE, TORAH, OR OTHER HOLY WORKS	Inscribe a personal note.
PERSONALIZED GIFTS	Create gifts such as personalized ceramics, furniture, or clothing. At arts and crafts stores, for example, you can paint your own cups, plates, or bowls, personalizing them to create lasting treasures. Peyton has made cups for Doug and me. Now we want to make something special for her.
FURNITURE	Attach notes that give the history of each piece and why you want the particular person to receive it.
JEWELRY	Pass down your favorite pieces of jewelry to both men and women. Men might particularly appreciate tie pins, pocket watches, rings or cufflinks.
SPORTING GOODS	Pass down favorite sporting goods. Doug has several treasures from his family—a pocketknife from his grandfather and a baseball mitt that his father used when they played catch together. They are clearly outdated, yet treasured heirlooms all the same.

TOOLS	For people who love tools, designate a toolbox or favorite tool for them to receive.
ADVANCE CARDS	If you are living with a serious illness, write letters or cards in advance of special events such as birthdays, holidays, Father's or Mother's Day, or to commemorate a future marriage or birth of a baby, etc. In the cards, add texture and meaning by sharing your own life experiences and feelings during similar special occasions.

❏ **Create a videotape or write a letter that expresses your love and encouragement for people who are dear to you.**

Later on, I talk about the videotapes I made for my daughter, Peyton. When I was busy taping them, Doug asked if I would record a videotape for him. I knew him better than anyone in the world, and he wanted to have a message from me that he could treasure forever. I loved the idea of creating a tape for him and wished I had thought of it myself! On my first tape for Doug, I talked about my happiest memories of our life together, including why I fell in love with him. I shared my hopes for him and my admiration for his unique qualities and talents. I talked about my beliefs in the afterlife and suggested people to whom he might turn for emotional support and counsel should I die before him.

➤ You can create a videotape for anyone you love. Here are some suggested topics:

1. Memories of growing up: childhood, teen years, reaching adulthood
2. Career choices, accomplishments, and failures
3. Financial mindset and practices
4. Educational history

5. Philosophies on: work, money, sports, education, religion, society, love
6. Favorites and why (Examples: color, food, movies, books, music, hobbies, art, season, adventures, trips, car)
7. Favorite memories together
8. Favorite traits of loved ones
9. What you most appreciate about loved ones

❏ **Encourage your loved ones to create emotional legacies for one another.**

In the process of dealing with my illness, Doug and I have both come to realize how precious life is. We have only one life, and as only God knows, Doug could pass away before I do. I have encouraged Doug to create his own diaries and recordings for our daughter. Doug is now creating his own video collection and personal history for Peyton.

IF YOU ARE A PARENT OR GRANDPARENT

❏ **Create audiotapes and videotapes of encouragement and assistance for your children or grandchildren.**

When I sat down to record my first videotape for Peyton, I cried each time I started talking. At first, I couldn't get over the idea that she might some day watch the videotapes without me. I had to restart the recorder several times before I was able to get my thoughts out without becoming overly emotional. What got me over the hump was realizing I had so much to tell her. For Peyton, I wanted to answer questions that children typically ask as they grow up. When I concentrated on all the positive messages I wanted to impart to her, the taping took on a much larger importance to me. I looked forward to thinking through what I wanted to say on each topic, creating the right frame of mind for the taping, setting up the machine, and speaking from my heart into the recorder.

➤ In creating audio- or videotapes for your children or grandchildren, I have several suggestions:

- Speak to the children as you would a friend, using words of encouragement and love.
- Choose your words carefully so you do not inadvertently create unrealistic expectations for your children. By this, I mean, be careful not to preach to them or set goals that will be impossible to attain.
- Talk about your life experiences, both positive and negative. Let your children know you hope they might learn from you and that you are not trying to tell them what to do. They will make their own choices in life, and your hope for them is to make good ones so they can live happy lives. Your thoughts would be just one of the influences on their future decisions.
- Let the children know that we all face choices in our lives and we benefit from (1) looking at life as a whole, and (2) keeping the end in mind when determining our priorities in life.

❏ **Decide what values and traits you would like to instill in your children or grandchildren.**

Before taping messages for our daughter, Doug and I talked at length about the values we wanted to instill in her, our hopes and dreams for her happiness (as opposed to our expectations), and our approach to some of the difficult issues that could come with the teen years. These conversations became a tremendous learning process for us both. By thinking ahead and articulating our thoughts on Peyton, we shifted how we interact with her day to day. For example, we discovered that a top priority for Peyton was for her to like and trust herself. While others might feel differently, for us, building Peyton's self-esteem came first. Knowing this, we found ourselves focused on empowering her to think for herself and articulate her own ideas and thoughts. We became more aware of nurturing her unique strengths and gifts. With our new approach, we saw Peyton beginning to absorb the lessons we wanted her to learn in life.

For us, if Peyton was to have both a good relationship with

God and positive self-esteem, all the other traits would naturally fall into place. Among the other traits we wanted to instill in her were

- Inner peace
- Honesty
- Integrity
- Follow-through
- Creativity
- Respect for the environment
- Respect for others, in particular respect for other cultures and religions

➤ Use this opportunity to think of the traits and values that are most important to you for the children. You might be surprised to find that articulating your specific long-term goals changes the way you interact with your children today.

❑ **Outline the topics for your taped or written messages to your children or grandchildren.**

From the beginning, my goal in developing the tapes has been for Peyton to know how loved she is. By taping and writing messages to her, I hoped to share ways of looking at problems or issues and to give her ideas that could open up new horizons for her. Ultimately, I let her know that the decisions were all hers. I did not want her to feel any pressure to fulfill some mandate of mine, or to feel needlessly constrained by the way I did things when I was young. This was her life to lead. I just wanted her to know some of the things I would have shared with her had I lived longer.

On the tapes I made for Peyton, rather than telling her what to do, I told her about my life and how I made my own decisions so that she might learn from me and about me. At the very least, through the tapes, I hoped she would get a better sense of who her mother was. For example, I made a recording on which I gave advice on choosing a husband. On that tape, I described how I listed, on a piece of paper, all the traits I hoped for in a husband and went into detail for her about each of these traits. I told her how, after completing the list, I realized that Doug had every one of the traits I was looking for. At the time, it was a revelation for me. It wasn't long thereafter that we started dating more seriously and I saw how much I loved him. Marrying him was one of the great decisions of my life.

On another tape, I suggested people she might turn to for advice on different topics, in case she wanted an opinion in addition to her dad's or grandparents'. I listed dear friends whom she could turn to for advice on topics ranging from finances to developing her relationship with God, handling difficult personalities, managing peer pressure, and even learning where to shop for bargains.

> ➤ It is important that a parent not try to "parent from the grave," but instead share thoughts and ideas in a loving and supportive way. Following is a list of tapes I made for Peyton when she was five years old. If your children are older, you will want to cover topics that are appropriate for their stage of development.

IMMEDIATE LOSS
(This tape is to be played within twenty-four hours of my death.)

I MISS MOMMY
- "Why did God take Mommy to Heaven?"
- "I am mad at Mommy for leaving."
- "My friend said that Mommy cannot hear me because she is in the ground."
- "What is Heaven like?"
- "Mommy still loves me."

REMARRIAGE
- "Will Daddy remarry?"
- "What would Mommy think?"
- "Will his new wife be my mother?"

GROWING UP/THE EARLY YEARS
- "What was my Mommy like?"
- "Who can I talk to about my problems?"
- "The girls are telling rumors about me and hurting my feelings."
- "I want to be liked."/Managing peer pressure
- Why doing drugs can close doors for you later in life
- You're not going crazy—your body is changing
- Your reputation and your name: your most valuable assets!
- A positive attitude is a daily choice.
- Relationships and team cooperation and leadership
- Personal discipline
- Financial responsibility

TEEN AND COLLEGE YEARS
- How to negotiate the purchase of your first car
- "Should I have sex with him?"
- "What college should I go to?"/"What should I major in?"
- Going to college
- Financing your education

AFTER COLLEGE
- "What job should I take?"
- "What should I do with my life?"
- "Should I marry him?"
- Maintaining a healthy marriage
- "Sometimes it is so hard to pray to God."
- "Should I have children?"
- "Raising children is sometimes very hard."

❏ **Create a videotape or write a letter on parenting issues for your spouse, partner or grown children.**
In addition to the videotape on which I shared what I loved most about Doug and my happiest memories of our life together, I recorded cassettes and videotapes for him on a variety of topics pertaining to parenting. On these tapes, I talked about building self-esteem in Peyton, helping to nurture her relationship with God, and other messages of encouragement. I hope these tapes will be a source of strength for Doug if I die from this disease. Following are the titles of the tapes I recorded for him (tapes covered more than one topic):

MY PASSING
- Immediate loss tape (to be played within twenty-four hours of my death)
- "Honey, I miss you. I feel so empty!"
- "It's so hard. I just want to be left alone with our daughter."
- "Why did God take you?"
- "I am so angry."
- Learning to balance time with Peyton and managing the responsibilities of the household
- Consistency and following through on promises

RAISING OUR DAUGHTER
- Heaven and God
- Schools
- Friends
- Nannies
- In-laws
- Activities/educational experiences
- Drugs
- Dating
- Teen pregnancy: Visit a home for pregnant teenagers.
- Teenage years

- First car
- Financial responsibility
- Inspiring her to be her own person

❏ **Create a wish list and book list for your children or grandchildren.**

Doug and I created wish lists for Peyton. In addition to the list of values and traits we wanted to instill in her, we identified experiences we wanted her to have and things we wanted her to learn in her lifetime. Also, I wrote down the books that had the greatest impact on me and which I hope my daughter will read before she turns eighteen. Again, our goal in creating these lists was not to try to impose our hopes and dreams on her. Quite the opposite. Our approach was to share our ideas and knowledge with her in hopes that she will find enjoyment and learning. At no point will we impose any activities or pursuits on her if she is not interested.

Among the things we hope she will do before she becomes an adult are to

- Learn to meditate
- Learn to play the piano and another musical instrument
- Speak a foreign language
- Take a course in Latin
- Take a self-defense course
- Learn how to negotiate for herself
- Learn how to budget
- Learn basic accounting and how to read financial statements
- Learn how to get a loan and build a positive credit rating
- Learn how to play sports of various kinds

In addition, we identified experiences we hope she might be interested in having, among them: river rafting, fishing, travelling internationally, being an exchange student, and creating and operating a small business at some point during her teenage years.

➤ We recommend talking together, as parents or grandparents, to create these wish lists. The conversations can be enlightening, and you might very well find yourself coming up with whole new ideas and activities you want to share with the children. Over time, these wish lists can serve as useful references for you in raising your children or grandchildren.

CHAPTER SUMMARY

❏ Organize and place your photographs in albums, and record audiotapes to be played while looking through the albums.

❏ Write letters to your loved ones telling them how much they mean to you.

❏ Keep a journal that might be shared with others in the event you pass away.

❏ Fill out a "Remember Book."

❏ Designate any items, such as jewelry, to be given to family members or friends on special occasions.

❏ Designate personal mementos or heirlooms to be given to family members or friends upon your death.

❏ Create a videotape or write a letter that expresses your love and encouragement for people who are dear to you.

❏ Encourage your loved ones to create emotional legacies for one another.

If You Are a Parent or Grandparent

❏ Create audiotapes and videotapes of encouragement and assistance for your children or grandchildren.

❏ Decide what values and traits you would like to instill in your children or grandchildren.

❏ Outline the topics for your taped or written messages to your children or grandchildren.

❏ Create a videotape or write a letter on parenting issues for your spouse, partner or grown children.

❏ Create a wish list and book list for your children or grandchildren.

3

PREPARE EMOTIONALLY:
LIVING WITH THE END IN MIND

~~❧❧~~

Preparing on an emotional level for your death is a different process if you are healthy than if you are ill. For me, reality set in over time and with my declining health. For Doug, although he has seen me come to terms with my illness and possible death from cancer, he could only guess at the circumstances of his own death and the emotions he might feel then. Like most strong and healthy people, he is focused on living, which is as it should be. Depending on when his time comes and whether he has advance warning, a whole range of emotions might rise to the surface. Until then, however, these emotions remain abstract notions.

What he has done, though, is to accept that at some point he and his loved ones will die. After spending his life ignoring this, Doug has had to come to terms with the possibility that, within a short period of time, he could lose the two adult women he loves most in the world. With his mother's death this year and the continuing uncertainties about my prognosis, the reality that death could be a long way off or just around the corner has finally hit home for him. We just don't know. As hard as this was to accept, and it's nearly impossible for me to fathom the sadness of his potential loss, Doug noticed a powerful shift in his perspective when he thought about living life with the end in mind.

For Doug, accepting mortality ultimately brought an enormous sense of clarity and confidence. He could make his life choices based on his deep-seated beliefs in what was important to him, what made him happy, and the impact he wanted to have on the world. Whereas before he would let inconsequential factors influence his decisions, he started cutting out unessential and uninteresting activities so that he could focus on his connection to God, the people he loved and the work that interested him. By living with the end in mind, Doug learned to be easier on himself, deepened his relationships with the people around him, and became more appreciative of the blessings in his life.

❏ **Accept that you will die and you probably don't know exactly when.**

Not long ago, a friend died while driving his car to the repair shop. His wife was following him in another car when he ran a stop sign and crashed into a house. She raced out of her car to see what was wrong, only to find him dead. He had had a heart attack.

So many of us go through life assuming we will live forever, and it's unsettling to think otherwise. Accepting one's mortality is easier said than done, however. One place to start is to ask yourself some questions:

1. If you knew you would die tomorrow, or a year from now, or five years from now, would you change your life as you lead it today?
2. What would it take for you to feel at peace with your life at the time of your death?

❏ **Tell your loved ones how important they are to you.**

After learning that my cancer was probably terminal, I asked myself, "Is there anything I would like to say to my family and friends that I would regret not having said if I were to pass away?"

The answer was immediate: I had a great deal I wanted to say and to hear from them as well. With some people, there were unresolved issues, past slights, or misunderstandings that I wanted to clear up. Other people had been very important to me earlier in my life, and we had lost touch over the years. With these, I wanted to reconnect. Overwhelmingly, though, I wanted my family members and friends to know how much I loved and treasured them.

At first, I was nervous because these conversations had the potential to mean so much. I wasn't accustomed to revealing my innermost feelings. As it turned out, I had no reason to worry. Talking with my family members and friends on this level was a discovery and a joy. We resolved issues from the past, cleared up misunderstandings, forgave each other, and laughed about our most treasured memories. We learned things about each other that we had never known before. I told them what I thought their greatest strengths were and thanked them for the great contributions they had made to my life. We had so much fun sharing ourselves during these conversations. It's funny, but confronting death allowed us to shake the cobwebs off our relationships so we could fully appreciate each other. Our relationships have been closer and more loving ever since.

Sometimes, though, these conversations took real effort. At one point, when Doug and I were feeling particularly disconnected and out of touch with each other, we scheduled an evening to talk just the two of us, without interruptions. At the time we were facing complex issues surrounding my illness and prognosis and had kept our feelings and fears all bottled up. Not knowing where to begin, we decided to let each other talk while the other listened, took notes and did not interrupt. Not interrupting was the hard part. Even when I mentioned worries or disappointments that applied to Doug directly, he let the information sink in and let me finish saying what I needed to say. When I had said everything, I did the same for him—just listened closely and tried to hear what he was feeling and grappling with. Then we talked together about what we had heard and the insights we had gained from each other.

Let me say that communicating on this level was not easy. It was difficult for me to hold my tongue when Doug relayed his worries about my possible death and having to manage on his own with Peyton, or his aggravation when the routines of our household were in chaos. While he was talking, I was tempted to jump into the conversation, try to fix things, make him feel better, and even defend myself. I had to remind myself that we needed to hear everything that was on each other's minds—the full weight of it—and then we could give each other comfort and come up with next steps. In the end, the process worked. It took two nights of talking to get through this first intense conversation, but the result was feelings of great relief and intimacy between us.

Some issues we raised could not be immediately remedied, but that was okay. We felt better just to have them out in the open, knowing we were on each other's side in dealing with them. With this exercise, we caught the first glimmer of what was to come—that we would find new ways to share ourselves and would come to feel closer and closer as my disease progressed and our ability to communicate improved. In some ways, the checklist started with these early conversations because, in them, we identified the most important and sometimes frightening issues we had to face. After articulating the issues, we set about tackling them.

➤ Telling your loved ones how much you care does not have to wait until you are on your deathbed or even terminally ill (assuming you are so lucky as to be given this advance time with your loved ones before you die). Grab the opportunity to reach out to your family and friends, preferably individually. Write down your feelings or ask them questions directly. For my friends, family, and me, it meant a great deal to express our feelings for one another, to relieve our consciences, or to say "I am sorry." Your friends and family need the opportunity to communicate their feelings while you are still living. Some questions you might ask yourself to get started are:

- Who are the people most important to me? Have I told them why I care so much about them?
- Are there people to whom I would like to say things (diplomatically and without hurting them) that I have never said before?
- What are the great strengths of the people around me?
- What important contributions have they made to my life? Have I acknowledged them recently for these contributions?
- What have I learned from them?
- Is there anything I would like to ask them?
- Is there anything I would like to request of them in the event I die before they do?
- Are there people I need to forgive or from whom I would like to receive forgiveness?

► Another approach is to write letters to loved ones, as Doug did for his parents' seventieth birthdays.

❑ **Accept your life for what it has been and what it is now.**
When I was growing up, my mother used to tell me and my siblings that we had to be able to look ourselves in the mirror. If we liked what we saw in ourselves, we would be doing okay. At the end of the day, we were responsible for our own characters, accountable to ourselves for our actions. Of course, there have been times when I have not liked what I have seen. Then, with Mom's words ringing in my head, I have had to do something about it—rethink my priorities, apologize to someone, or resolve to act differently in the future.

► Too many people live with regrets, allowing their remorse to eat away at them. Whatever regret, sorrow, or unfulfilled dream might be stealing the vigor and excitement from your life today, there comes a time for acceptance and moving on. Sometimes, you might need a period of mourning, or to forgive yourself or others before you can relinquish nagging feelings, but the point is to *want* to get over whatever has dragged you down. If you need to have conversations with other people or talk to a counselor to get over whatever feelings are eating away at you, do so. Get whatever support you need, with an eye toward resolving issues in a timely way. The point is to move on and enjoy the life that remains ahead of you.

❏ Take responsibility for your happiness.

Doug and I recently woke up to the fact that aspects of Doug's life have been on hold for four years. On one level, he had taken care of me and Peyton in addition to shouldering the financial burdens of the household. On another, deeper level, Doug knew I might die from this disease and had organized his priorities around what he thought I wanted for my last years. At some point along the way, he started ignoring his own life goals. Not long ago, I began to see a sadness about him. He was giving all he could and was becoming completely drained. Being ill, I needed his love and attention, but as a wife who loves her husband, I did not like what I saw—my life at the expense of his. We talked about this, and little by little, Doug has taken more time for himself and we have integrated his priorities and interests back into our lives.

➤ Do not let other people's priorities overshadow your life goals. Many people, for example, let their careers dominate their lives, spending decades focused entirely on work, while their families, friends, and interests sit on the back burner. After years of living one-dimensional lives, these people can lose touch with what makes them feel happy and fulfilled. Think about what makes you happy, and organize your life to allow time for what you enjoy. Doug uses the analogy of driving a car. You can sit in the back seat and let life drive you—meaning you can let your schedule and the constant demands on your time dictate your priorities. Or you can take the steering wheel and be responsible for your own happiness, knowing that you are the one who ultimately is accountable for whether you are happy or not.

❏ Forgive yourself and others.

When I was younger, one of my dearest friends betrayed my trust. Since then, we remained in touch and still loved each other, but our friendship suffered because this unspoken incident stood between us. When my cancer spread, we had a long talk about what had happened all those years ago. She brought it up because she had felt so guilty ever since. As we talked, the incident became insignificant. It was such a weight off our shoulders to forgive each other—to just let the incident go. Now when I think about it, I remember what happened, but I don't feel the sadness or anger that I had felt, and our relationship has been transformed. We feel even closer and more intimate than ever before.

➤ Forgiveness means letting go of the anger or hurt that has driven a wedge between you and other people. Forgiveness sounds simple, but it can be very difficult. Some issues can seem too big for forgiveness. Terrible hurts or injustices can fester and gnaw at a person until the whole world seems tainted. In the end, though, we all have a choice. We can let ourselves continue to feel hate or anger, or we can forgive and find peace.

➤ We all know of unhappy souls who continuously point to the pains inflicted on them in their childhood as the source of their despair as adults. Forgiveness and choosing to move on in life can create whole new openings for happiness. Choose to be in the present and celebrate all its beauty.

❏ **Give to others.**

After the cancer spread to my spine, Doug and I withdrew from our circle of friends and family. We had so much on our plates—my disease, Doug's job, raising our daughter, keeping our household going. We just put our heads down and tried to get everything done. We became so focused on ourselves that our lives started to feel dull and uninspiring. We reached a point where we felt stagnant. What was missing was that positive feeling that comes with reaching out to others, even in small ways. With no love flowing out, there was very little room to feel the love coming our way either. To change that, we found ways to celebrate the special occasions of friends and family members, we reached out to friends who were sick or hurting, and we tried to be better listeners for our loved ones who needed our support. The more love we gave away, the more we received.

➤ A great way to balance your emotional and spiritual sides is to give of yourself to others who are also in need. Love must stay in motion to remain fresh and alive. When we give to others, we truly receive.

❏ **Give your spouse permission to marry again.**

When I first told Doug that I hoped he would remarry if I died, he said, "No way." He was not interested in ever marrying again. What we had was too special; he could not imagine himself with another woman. Over the years, I have occasionally asked him to keep an open mind to the concept for three reasons: (1) If I were to pass away today, we would have been married for ten years. He still could conceivably find someone and be married for fifty more years. (2) If God would bless him with the opportunity to love again, that would be a precious gift. And (3) If God so provided, it would be my great wish for Peyton to have a female influence and second mother. By having these conversations with Doug, I wanted him to know that he would not betray his memory of me if he were to love again with all his heart. He eventually said he would at least consider the idea of remarrying if I died, though the prospect still seemed far-fetched.

I also recorded an audiotape for Peyton if Doug started dating or decided to remarry (Doug could decide at the time if he wanted to give the tape to Peyton). I told her I trusted Daddy's judgment to bring someone into the household who was a caring and loving person. I said that if Daddy chose to remarry, I would bless the marriage. It would be up to Daddy to decide if he wanted to marry again, and that his possible wife might or might not feel like a mother to Peyton, but my hope was that she would. It would be up to Peyton and Daddy's new wife to define their relationship, but I hoped that Peyton and she would have a loving and nurturing relationship together. I also talked about how Peyton might manage the changing dynamic of the household if Daddy remarried and his future wife had other children.

➤ Let your spouse know that you feel it would be a blessing for him or her to fall in love again, that you bless the sacrament of a future marriage. I recommend carefully sharing your feelings about this with your children. My preferred approach is to record a tape or write a letter that can be shared with the children at a later time. That way, if the time comes, your children will be more inclined to accept the new person into their lives. It is a good idea to share your feelings on this topic with your parents and in-laws as well.

❏ **Identify and join an organization that offers social activities, particularly around holidays.**

Throughout our marriage, I have been the one to reach out to friends and arrange social activities. Doug is just not as good at making social plans (unless an event involves sports or coworkers). This has worried me a bit. Since he was not accustomed to initiating social events and activities, Doug might feel cut off from his friends if something happened to me. Certainly, the transition to handling this on his own would be difficult. So for us, the answer was to join a sports club. The club offered several sports Doug enjoyed and a natural environment for him to make new friends. For Peyton, the club had activities and sponsored events in celebration of most holidays.

> ➤ I recommend taking the time to integrate your spouse, partner, or loved one into a club or association of some kind, especially if your spouse is not by nature a social person. This is particularly important if you are the one who usually makes the social arrangements for the family. Churches, synagogues, and clubs can be particularly supportive with their holiday celebrations and other festivities throughout the year.

IF YOU ARE A PARENT OR GRANDPARENT

After learning that my cancer was probably terminal, Doug and I decided we wanted to prepare Peyton in small ways for the possibility that she might lose her mother. Over a period of several years, since Peyton was two years old, Doug and I have allowed conversations about life and death to unfold at a natural pace. Our approach with Peyton has been to treat conversations about life and death much like any other discussion, without added seriousness or consternation. Mostly, we took our cues from her. For example, when Peyton found a cicada shell in the backyard, I showed her how the cicada had left the shell behind after removing itself from the shell and flying off. I compared this to when we die: I explained how our spirits leave our bodies and leave behind our physical shells and go to heaven. As humans, we bury the body (or shell) in remembrance of the person whose spirit has gone to heaven.

We knew if we were nervous or uncomfortable talking with her about life and death issues, she would pick up on it. In particular, if we appeared scared, she would get scared. Given my uncertain health, we could not avoid the topic entirely because that could create anxiety for everyone. So, before talking to Peyton, Doug and I worked together to figure out what we wanted to say to her. We wanted to avoid the conventional euphemisms one associates with conversations about death. Instead, we wanted to speak from the heart and share our views in such a way that she gained her own understanding of death as a part of life.

Since we had a lot of thinking to do, Doug and I decided to take a weekend to reflect on our beliefs and approaches. Close friends in Colorado let us borrow their condo, and we settled in with pads of paper, a laptop computer, and lots of ideas and quiet time. We started out talking about our views on death, life after death, and our fears. We each wrote what we had learned about ourselves and our views of the world since discovering I had cancer. We talked about living—and even parenting—with the end in mind; we tried imagining Peyton reaching her full potential as an adult. For example, we decided we wanted Peyton to have high self-esteem. From there, we worked backward to the present. How could our parenting best support her to become the person she was meant to be? As we looked at this question, we realized our focus had been on controlling the behavior of our child rather than empowering her. We could try to control her or we could empower her to think for herself and articulate her own ideas and thoughts. As parents, we decided our role was to nurture her unique strengths and gifts. Within this context of parenting with the end in mind, we came up with ways of talking about death and dying that would seem neither frightening nor abstract to her.

Looking back over these years, I marvel that these beautiful and life-affirming conversations with Peyton occurred only because I was terminally ill. If we had not talked about life and death in a way she could understand at a young age, her first exposure to death would have been when a relative or friend died. What a disservice to Peyton! I have come to believe that loving parents should talk with their young children about death as a natural occurrence in life. That way, as the child grows into adulthood (or if the child loses a loved one), death will not seem so traumatic and frightening.

It is important to note that we have been careful not to overemphasize the topic of death. We have had years to develop our checklist and have talked with Peyton about life-and-death issues only when the moment was right for her. If we had talked too much about death and dying, Peyton could have become worried or preoccupied with thoughts about death. Rushing into these discussions or placing too much importance on the subject would have been terribly counterproductive.

➤ Please take your time when working on this chapter. Don't rush into things with your children or grandchildren. Let them have time to react and digest new information. Listen to any concerns they might have and respond with love and sensitivity.

➤ For those of you who are battling a terminal illness, you will have to strike your own balance when covering these topics with your children or grandchildren. We have some suggestions in this chapter, but ultimately, you know your children and how best to communicate with them. As I suggest later in this chapter, you may want to talk with a professional counselor who could coach you before your discussions with your children or grandchildren.

❏ **For your grown children, address issues associated with death and dying.**

As for adult children, never underestimate the "child" in all of us. None of us, no matter the age, is prepared for the death of a loving parent. I have repeatedly heard of older people who wanted to discuss their plans for their eventual death, but their adult children would have nothing to do with the conversation. If this has been your experience, it may be best to write down your thoughts and feelings about important points raised in this checklist and give the document to your adult children so that over time they can reread and fully absorb your opinions and wishes.

❏ **Be prepared for questions your young children or grandchildren might ask about death and dying.**
Out of curiosity, most young children will occasionally ask questions about death. Given my health, Doug and I wanted to be particularly clear and consistent in the event that Peyton asked questions about death in general or about my longevity specifically. As I mentioned before, first Doug and I talked about our beliefs and how we wanted to impart these to Peyton. Then we did some reading. We found excellent child development books on how children of different ages comprehend death. We also talked to several child psychologists who specialize in child development and grieving. We learned that some experts think children up to the age of six view death as reversible, magical, something that occurs in a far-off time, or they think the dead person can still interact in some way. By the age of six, children start to have a more realistic understanding of death. By the age of nine, most children have an adult understanding of what death means. Doug and I found it very helpful to know how children of different ages process information and create meaning for themselves so that we could tailor our discussions with Peyton accordingly.

When Peyton asked questions, we followed a simple formula. We answered her simply and directly, without going overboard with details. If she wanted to talk more, we encouraged her questions. If answering the one question was enough for her, we let the topic drop. If she said something about death that we thought was wrong, we corrected her. And we made sure she did not see death as a punishment of any kind. Several questions we knew she probably would ask at some point were:

- Who will take care of me if you die?
- What happens when people die? Where do people go when they die?

- When will I die? When will you die?
- Why do people die?
- Do people die because God is unhappy with them?
- What is heaven like?
- Will we see each other in heaven?

➤ Write down the questions your children might ask about death, and think through your answers. It will come as a relief to be prepared for the questions your children ask and not feel stumped when they spontaneously ask questions that you can't answer off the top of your head. I recommend talking to counselors to get their advice on answering the questions your children might ask.

➤ If you don't know the answer to questions your children ask, just say so. There aren't answers to everything in this world. Or you can say, "Let me think about that." Then you can answer the question the next day, after you have had time to think about your answer. It's far better to be honest than to give your children answers that may cause them to become confused.

❏ **Introduce the concept of death and dying to your children or grandchildren in ways that are sensitive to their maturity and emotional response.**

Every child is unique. Depending on a child's age, maturity, and emotional development, he or she will react differently to conversations about life and death. For Peyton, since she was two years old, we have gauged our conversations according to her level of understanding and interest. For example, she has asked more complicated questions as a six-year-old than she did as a two-year-old, and we have adjusted our explanations. Most important, our primary focus has been on her overall development and happiness, with these conversations about life and death coming up only rarely. We are pleased that Peyton seems to have a comfortable understanding of the circle of life and the concept of death. If she were ever to show any signs of confusion, unhappiness, or anger, we would regroup and update our approach.

> Before talking with your children about life-and-death issues, take into consideration their ages, emotional maturity, stability, development levels, and personalities. Be prepared to adapt your discussions based on the ever-changing needs of your children.

❏ **Casually drive through the cemetery of your choice with your children or grandchildren so it is familiar.**

We took our daughter to the cemetery on a beautiful spring day to talk about the burial process. A burial was taking place nearby, and we pointed out the different stages of funerals. We said, "Look, someone already went to heaven and now they are burying the body in remembrance of them." We talked again about heaven and the example of the cicada shell. We talked about how, if any of us were to die, our souls would leave our bodies and go to heaven. Then, from heaven, we would look over our family members on earth.

❏ **If you are comfortable with the concept, attend a funeral with your children or grandchildren and explain what is occurring.**

Doug and I attended a funeral for a friend who had recently passed away from breast cancer and left behind a five-year-old and a three-year-old. We brought Peyton, who was four years old, so we could explain what was happening. We talked about the funeral service and the burial process and explained that everyone was gathered to celebrate the life of our friend. We pointed out that we would all miss her very much, especially her family. By introducing our daughter to the cemetery and the burial process in our terms and controlled time frame, we hoped to lessen the potential shock for Peyton of seeing one of her parents buried in an unfamiliar process and place. (If the child is younger, I suggest you avoid viewing an open casket.)

➤ Attending a funeral with your children will help get them familiar with the process of saying good-bye to someone. I have adult friends whose parents kept them from attending a funeral when my friends were young. Only as adults did they realize they had missed out on a fundamental passage of life. I have come to believe that sharing with children an appreciation for the full circle of life can give them a tool to help them deal with their own grief, when they in turn lose someone they love.

❏ **Emphasize the circle of life to your children and grand-children.**

We balanced these comments with assurances to Peyton that she will probably live a long life on earth filled with great adventures and beautiful purpose. We emphasized celebrating the circle of life, including life and death. Peyton and I have talked about her great-grandparents who are in heaven and looking over us now. We went into detail about her great-grandparents' lives so she could imagine them as real people who lived full lives on earth. Then, we talked about her future children and grandchildren and about how someday she would go to heaven and look over her children and her children's children. We made the concept uplifting and full of love. Her response was fabulous. She loved the thought of being looked after by her great-grandparents in heaven and of someday looking after her own children and grandchildren from heaven. This order in the world helped give her an appreciation for her life as part of a much larger circle of life.

➤ Care should be taken so that your children or grandchildren see their lives in the appropriate context. They cannot realize their full potential if they artificially truncate their lives (by committing suicide) to be with someone who has died. Cutting one's own life short is a tragedy that is inconsistent with the circle of life. Instead, children should focus on making their lives full, long, and productive.

❏ **If someone close to your children or grandchildren dies or is dying, inform others of your discussions with them.**
When Doug's mother died, we talked with the adults in Peyton's life about conversations we had had with Peyton about her grandmother's death. Our goal was for her remaining grandparents, her caregiver, and the other important adults in her life to be consistent so Peyton would not get mixed messages. At the time, she was only five years old and did not entirely understand what death was. So, in keeping with her age and maturity, we made our explanation simple and uncomplicated.

We talked about her grandmother's death by acknowledging the sadness of her grandmother being physically gone from the family while feeling the joy of:

1. Grandma being with God and feeling all of His love;
2. Grandma being without pain in heaven;
3. Grandma watching over the family from heaven; and
4. The whole family being together again in heaven one day.

Peyton was so young that she did not dwell on the subject for long periods of time, but came back to it periodically. It was especially helpful in the days following my mother-in-law's death (when Peyton occasionally talked about her grandmother or asked questions) that the other adults in Peyton's life reinforced our conversations and approach.

➤ This is an age-appropriate consideration. If your children are much older than Peyton, conversations about death and dying can be more involved and multifaceted. No matter the age, it is important to tell them exactly what has occurred, simply and directly, and then be a good listener, ready to respond to their needs. As with adults, children react differently to death. For some, it takes longer for the information to sink in, so they might at first appear unfazed by the news. Others might immediately become very emotional upon hearing of the death. There is no right way or wrong way to react.

❏ **If someone close to your children or grandchildren dies or is dying, allow your children to grieve in their own way.** Grieving is hard, whether we are young or old, and we all do it differently. Children sometimes cope in ways that can be surprising to adults. Often, for example, children will be sad for a short time and then will go play and laugh. Adults can become upset by this because they think the children are exhibiting a callous disregard for the sadness of the occasion, when in truth the children are coping by doing what is familiar to them. A friend recalled her reactions to her mother's death when my friend was very young:

> *I cried for two hours after my mother died and then I went outside to play. This upset my grandmother terribly, but it was how I needed to handle it. Other family members need to be aware of a child's grief process—and that each child is different. I remember being asked if I even missed my mother. Of course I did, but children process grief and death so much differently.*[1]

➤ Grief is not limited to the time after a person dies; "anticipatory grief" can occur before a person dies if there is a long decline before death. We suggest the following guidelines for helping children grieve:[2]

- Be there and share in the grief.
- Give your love and support and understanding.
- Know that it is okay to cry.
- Listen.

---

1. Lori Abernathy.
2. Susan Istre, Ph.D.

- Do not force undue questioning, but rather, answer any questions your children raise themselves.
- If the child expresses guilt or responsibility, correct the child in a firm and caring way.
- Don't overtalk and suggest things they can do to feel better.
- Allow the child to express what he or she needs from you; then respond to that need.
- Follow the normal routine as much as possible.
- Maintain discipline and limits.
- Don't overindulge the child to try to "make up" for the loss.
- Allow and be alert for questions related to loss.
- Understand that your child might need more attention for a while.
- Be watchful for behavior that may indicate a need for special support (i.e., poor academic performance, apathy, punishment-seeking behaviors, changes in values, spreading rumors).

CHAPTER SUMMARY

❑ Accept that you will die and you probably don't know exactly when.
❑ Tell your loved ones how important they are to you.
❑ Accept your life for what it has been and what it is now.
❑ Take responsibility for your happiness.
❑ Forgive yourself and others.
❑ Give to others.
❑ Give your spouse permission to marry again.
❑ Identify and join an organization that offers social activities, particularly around holidays.

If You Are a Parent or Grandparent
❑ For your grown children, address issues associated with death and dying.

❐ Be prepared for questions your young children or grand-children might ask about death and dying.

❐ Introduce the concept of death and dying to your children or grandchildren in ways that are sensitive to their maturity and emotional response.

❐ Casually drive through the cemetery of your choice with your children or grandchildren so it is familiar.

❐ If you are comfortable with the concept, attend a funeral with your children or grandchildren and explain what is occurring.

❐ Emphasize the circle of life to your children and grand-children.

❐ If someone close to your children or grandchildren dies or is dying, inform others of your discussions with them.

❐ If someone close to your children or grandchildren dies or is dying, allow your children to grieve in their own way.

4

WHEN ILLNESS STRIKES: FINDING YOUR EMOTIONAL BALANCE

After *20/20* did a story on this checklist, I received letters and E-mail messages from people across the country. One message particularly struck me:

> *"I lost my wife . . . to cancer [last year]. We took a different path. [My wife] believed that a positive attitude and carrying on with life as if the disease was an inconvenience was the way to a cure. The results were a living nightmare for her and still are for me—love and best friends lost, family destroyed, convictions and beliefs shattered, denial, financial ruin, life's work and legacy stolen . . . I do not blame her for anything. I know that she believed that what she was doing would save her life. I know that she would never hurt anyone. However, I now believe that not taking the steps that Mrs. Kramp has taken destroyed her final days and have left the survivors scarred for life."*

I have seen many families torn apart by the emotional ramifications of a serious illness. Addressing the emotional issues associated with disease can be very difficult. What Doug and I have found, though, is that life doesn't get any easier by living in denial—it gets harder. When we refused to acknowledge how sick I was and did not face up to my physical limitations, our stress levels increased enormously. We stopped communicating with each other and friends, and we got more and more frightened about our situation. Meetings with doctors became a major test because we could not bear to hear bad news. Only when we talked together about what we were up against—individually, as a couple, as a family, with our friends—did the stress ease up and our lives come into focus. For us, communication and preparation were the two most important tools for handling the emotional aspects of being seriously ill.

❏ **Notify loved ones of your illness.**

After finding a lump in my breast when I was on a skiing trip with friends, I went to see several doctors who said I had nothing to worry about. Since the lump was small, and I was only thirty-one, some of the doctors advised against removing it. Doug and I didn't agree with them. After much discussion we decided we wanted the lump taken out because we did not like the thought that there was something foreign in my body. Dr. Richard Anderson, a family friend, agreed that the safest option was to remove the lump surgically.

For the meeting with Dr. Anderson following the surgery, at the last minute, my mother decided to join Doug and me. (Call it a mother's intuition.) Together we were stunned by his pronouncement that I had cancer, as were our family and friends when we told them. None of us could quite believe it. Ultimately, my disease became a catalyst for my family members, friends, and me to communicate with one another on a whole new level. But the news of my illness did not immediately spark the deep and meaningful communication that came later. Actually quite the opposite.

My sister, Debbi, says that crises tend to exaggerate people's natural inclinations, which is what initially happened within my family. Everyone reacted differently to my illness, and no one was entirely comfortable with anyone else's distinct approaches. For example, my parents, Doug, and I handled the news by focusing on finding the right specialists and researching treatment options. Although we each had our emotional moments, we primarily went into problem-solving mode, researching everything we could learn about the disease. For some time, I was matter-of-fact and businesslike, and hid beneath a mountain of work.

Some of my other family members and friends tended to be more emotional as they grappled with the diagnosis. Some went into denial, a few wanted be very involved in discussing my treatment options, while others thought they should let me have my privacy and not intrude. My family had always been exceptionally close-knit, but according to my siblings, not long after my diagnosis, they felt somewhat at odds with each other; someone was being too stoic, someone else wasn't helping out enough or was being too emotional. Amazingly, my siblings had appreciated each other's differences in the past, but with this crisis, they began to feel disconnected from one another. In my brother Michael's opinion, "We went from being a family that could have been on a Wheaties cereal box to one that would better represent Froot Loops." For a time, things were a bit loopy, but we did not know what to do about it.

It wasn't until after my cancer metastasized that my family members got together at various times to talk about my prognosis and how the family was coping. My sister Noreen told me afterward that it was during these informal family gatherings that they gave one another permission to react in their own unique ways to my illness and my possible death. No one had the right answer, and they realized their job was to support and love each other during the tough times. As a group, they decided they would not judge each other or try to impose their views on one another.

Our relationships with one another have given me indescribable strength. By contemplating life and death and sharing our feelings and insights, we have become even closer than we had been before. We have had incredible, unforgettable conversations that changed the way we looked at the world and each other.

Ultimately, my relationships with the ones I love have become the richest and most important dimension of my life, and I would not necessarily have known that if I hadn't shared the news of my illness. If I had kept the news of the cancer to myself I don't know how I would have survived.

Looking back, I am certain that the love and prayers of my family and friends have kept me alive for so long. The intimacy we now share with one another is just one of the reasons that I consider cancer to have been a gift to me.

➤ Tell your family members and friends that you are terminally ill. Sharing this information is an unselfish act. The people in your life need time to adjust to the fact that you might not be with them for long.

➤ Your family and friends want to let you know how much they care about you, and they want to help. Although you might think, "I know they love me," they need to know that you know. Your family and friends need an opportunity to express themselves. The gift of knowing in advance of your possible death should not be wasted, but celebrated. Friends and family express their love in different ways—by sharing their hearts, writing cards, and even running errands or making dinner.

➤ Keeping your illness to yourself is anxiety producing. I believe the stress associated with such solitude is detrimental to one's health and may actually further the progression of disease. Reach out to your relations, friends, and coworkers.

❑ **Allow yourself to be pleasantly surprised by the people in your life.**

Without having told family and friends about my illness, Doug and I never would have discovered how deeply caring so many people are. Certainly, some people were uncomfortable around illness and did not know how to react, but others have been incredibly loving and supportive. I have been consistently surprised by the ones who have taken time to reach out and make a special effort. If we were to mention all the incredible things people have done for us, this checklist item would be the size of an encyclopedia! Countless times, friends and family members have shown up at a moment's notice to support us through our never-ending crises. Friends and family have stayed the weekend with me, brought meals to the house, written beautiful letters, and even composed poems and produced songs. And then, the most incredible gifts have been the prayers of our family, friends, and acquaintances.

➤ It might take some time to adjust and let people help and support you, as it did for us. Know that people want to help and their involvement in your life is an opportunity to enrich and deepen your relationships. You might even discover new depths to the people in your life—as we did.

❑ **Learn how to receive from friends and strangers.**

This was hard for Doug and me. Having thought of ourselves as self-sufficient people all our adult lives, we found it difficult to let others do so much for us. On top of that, I felt terribly guilty that people were giving so much when I could give so little in return. I am still grappling with these feelings of guilt and frustration at not being able to do more for myself and having to rely on others. At least I have stopped saying, "You shouldn't have gone to all that trouble." Instead, I have tried my best to let people know how much I appreciate their involvement in our lives and their help with everything from the mundane chores around the house, taking me to the doctors, and preparing food for me.

❑ **Let people know how they can help you.**

Doug and I have most appreciated the people who don't ask us what we need, but anticipate what we might need or enjoy: a dinner prepared for an evening following a visit to the doctors; a special activity arranged for Peyton when I am not feeling my best;

organizing my chaotic house when I have been bedridden. When people ask what they can do to help, it often is difficult to tell them without feeling as if we are imposing on friendships. (My suggestion: when people ask what they can do, mention some of the following things that friends and family members have done for us.)

- Form a meal team to deliver meals to your home. One person coordinates the group, keeping track of the names, phone numbers, addresses, and dishes brought to your home. Suggestions for the meal team:
  —Ask your dietary preferences.
  —Deliver food in disposable containers that do not need to be returned.
  —Include paper plates so that other dishes don't have to be used.
- Create a phone chain so that loved ones can receive updates on your health without your having to call everyone. To organize a phone chain, write a list of family members and friends who want to participate. Send each one a copy of the list. When the first person on the list receives a call, he or she calls the next person on the list, and on down the line until everyone knows the latest news.
- Form a transportation committee to drive you to and from the doctor's office or the hospital.
- Write an update letter, address and mail it to friends and family (after you read it over and give your sign off).
- Handle your medical insurance claims (one of the most demanding and frustrating aspects of having a serious illness).
- Conduct research and collect newspaper and journal articles for you to read on your illness and treatment options.
- Be in charge of laughter. (I have designated a friend, who loves to laugh and always seems to have something funny to say, to be the person I turn to when I need a good chuckle. When I call her, I can count on her to tell me a joke or share with me the latest funny story.)

- Call when they are running errands to see if you need anything.
- Buy a fresh article of clothing or something else to perk you up. Examples: a scarf, shirt, pajamas, robe, new sheets, towels, lotions, aromatherapy, music, or dried flower arrangements (it's sometimes difficult to breathe with poignant flowers around).
- Offer to:
  —Clean your house or fix up the yard.
  —Read out loud, buy a book on tape, or rent a video.
  —Take you for a ride in the car to see the outdoors.
  —Straighten out closets or do spring cleaning.
  —Take your children for a day so you can have some free time.
  —Write checks to pay bills.
  —Give blood, should you need transfusions.

➤ Everyone has their own unique strengths when helping you out. For example, my sister Noreen is very good at making a home reflect the season, and has regularly decorated our house so we would feel in the holiday spirit. My sister Debbi, who is an inventive chef, came up with recipes for foods I could digest during times when the side effects of chemotherapy were most debilitating. My brother, Michael, who has a wonderful way with words, has written me poems that boost my spirits and has helped me with various writing projects.

❏ **Communicate with your loved ones.**

In many ways, Doug reacted to my diagnosis much as I did. He became distracted by wanting to find a cure and by trying to maintain a normal family life. We put up a strong front, which blocked out the emotional implications of what was happening in our lives. At one point, after particularly bad news from my doctor, I realized things had gone too far. It was unhealthy to keep everything all bottled up. I wasn't sure how to break through our "we-can-handle-anything" facades. In fact, I became so concerned about Doug's and my pent-up emotions that I invited him to see the movie *Shadowlands*, at the theater (without telling him the subject matter). If you have not seen it, *Shadowlands* beautifully depicts the true story of C. S. Lewis and Joy Gresham, played by Anthony Hopkins and Debra Winger, and their love for each other as they cope with Joy's terminal cancer. After the movie ended, we both wept in the parking lot. We just cried and cried about the sadness of it all. It was a tremendous catharsis to cry out our anguish and hold each other. Since then, we have tried to give ourselves opportunities to let our emotions rise to the surface, without having to resort to my luring Doug to the movies. (Since then, Doug has been more cautious when I have suggested going to the movies!) Our experience has been that the most powerful tool for managing the pressures and lightening the load is communication.

> ➤ When there is a crisis in a family, the stresses on the family and friends can be tremendous. Relationships can break down, anxiety levels can rise, and depression can set in. The healthiest thing you can do for yourself during difficult times is to find someone to whom you can completely express your emotions (preferably someone over the age of eighteen).

❏ **Reach your own peace with your illness.**

Shortly after learning of my diagnosis, I set about trying to figure out why I had the disease. Doug has laughed at me numerous times, recalling my first interaction with the doctors when I learned I had cancer. I was wheeled out of the recovery room and, already I had a pen and paper in hand and was grilling the doctors and nurses on everything they could tell me about breast cancer. Basically, my rationale was, if I could understand the disease, even find a cause, then I could control it. I was terribly afraid of the unknown and wanted to be able to plan an effective counterattack to the disease. Since there was no history of cancer in my family, I felt there had to be another reason. I fixated on my diet, eating organic foods and macrobiotic cooking. (My sister-in-law, Lisa, even took cooking classes so she could cook macrobiotic meals for me.) I had my house tested for electromagnetic fields (and had several electrical outlets rewired when I learned they were emitting these fields). Our family stopped using a microwave oven because we did not know if the microwaves could possibly interfere with the integrity of the food. I thoroughly researched the disease, the specialists and their success rates, and the conventional and alternative treatments that offered the greatest hope.

Eventually, I realized that environmental factors might have contributed to my contracting cancer, but I would never know with any certainty. Not finding answers was very hard on me. I had to accept the idea that treating cancer was not an exact science and that, as a society, we had a long way to go before cancer would be universally understood and treatable. There was no simple explanation for why I had the disease, which meant there were no sure cure-alls. After a lot of hard work and anxious soul searching, I finally decided all I could do was take the best care of me I knew how. That meant eating well, living as clean and stress-free a life as possible, surrounding myself with loved ones and prayer, and using radiation and chemotherapy.

❏ **Create a strategy for treating your illness.**

Deciding to use radiation and chemotherapy led to the most emotionally charged conversation I had with Doug and my parents since cancer struck four years ago. For a long time, I resisted using chemotherapy because, fundamentally, I saw it as an antiquated treatment. Fighting off a disease by killing the immune system just did not make sense to me. Besides, the statistical evidence showed that chemotherapy had a marginal chance of curing the cancer. According to my findings, I might live the same amount of time whether or not I used chemotherapy. While I was researching the conventional treatment options, I heard countless anecdotes from people who had survived cancer using alternative treatments. There was no hard evidence in support of these treatments, just lots of heartfelt stories that were very convincing. At one point, I decided I would use alternative treatments and not use chemo, and told my husband and parents of my decision.

They were horrified. Doug, Mom, and Dad were convinced I would die if I did not use chemo. They argued that chemotherapy was the only protocol the doctors offered that had been shown to work consistently for some people. The next night, the four of us had a conversation, during which I asked Doug to decide for me. I was paralyzed by my dislike for chemo and my uncertainties about the alternative treatments. Doug decided on the chemo, which scared him too. There was enough evidence to show that chemo could kill me before the cancer did. My friends who chose not to do chemotherapy when I did but relied solely on holistic medicines have since passed away.

Settling on my approach to treating the disease was an enormous relief. Of course, I have kept a sharp eye out for any new conventional and alternative treatments that offered promise, yet I no longer have felt that a battle was waging inside me to find answers that weren't there to be found.

I have tried to integrate the best of both the conventional and alternative treatments, as have many of my friends. For example, I have relied on a friend, Sharon Kraus, an acupuncturist, to help control my nausea and pain, and to counterbalance the detrimental side effects of chemotherapy. She has even come to my home in the middle of the night to administer to me when the pain was so great that I otherwise would have had to go to the hospital. As more becomes known about both conventional and alternative approaches, it seems inevitable that physicians will find new ways to combine treatments so as to manage the health of the whole person, rather than focusing so exclusively on the cancerous growths.

❑ Address your fears about death.

My first real experience with death was as a seventh grader when my grandfather passed away. At the memorial service, I cried so uncontrollably I had to be removed from the service. I missed him terribly. The fear of death has always plagued me, but never for myself. My fears always revolved around the pain associated with losing someone I loved. I was so mortified at the prospect of losing someone that, as a child, I asked God to take me before he took my father. At the time, I was worried about Dad because he was working so hard and traveling so much. It was much easier for me to imagine myself dying than him, particularly if he were to leave my mother before they had a chance to enjoy each other in their retirement years. They had both worked hard to raise the family and provide for us. For as long as I can remember, I was willing to die before a loved one died. Some may call that unselfish. I think otherwise. I was frightened of the loss.

After receiving my diagnosis, I finally had to face the reality of death. I would sometimes lie awake at night with questions and fears about my possible death. These episodes were often frightening and emotionally draining. Crying late at night would only make me feel worse. What I discovered, though, was that each fear would haunt me until I addressed it and resolved it for myself. I had to shine the light of day on each fear and figure out how to get past it. Once I examined the fear and came up with my own answers, often after talking with other people, whatever had scared me disappeared. In its place I felt peace—until the next fear popped up. One by one, I worked through the fears and the worries until there were no more.

Amazingly, I found it was much harder to ignore my fears than to confront them. All the effort that went into working up my courage to confront a new fear took much more out of me than actually facing the fears head on. Hiding and running away didn't work. I began to see that this was like facing any challenge, whether it be giving a big presentation or jumping off the high dive for the first time. As a friend advised me, "Move toward your anxiety." When I did, my anxieties stopped manipulating my emotions. In their place was peace of mind—without the nagging voice in my head droning on about the implications of my possible death.

Though we all have our own unique fears about death, mine centered on four themes. I feared: (1) leaving my loved ones; (2) incomplete business; (3) fear of no life after death; and (4) the actual process of dying. I will briefly describe how I addressed each of these fears for myself.

• **Fear of leaving my loved ones.** This was my biggest fear and remains so. I did not want to give up all the love we shared. I worried about leaving without having showed my family and friends how much I loved them. I worried about how my family would get by without me. And I was frightened for Peyton growing up without me as her mother. I felt I was the best mother she could have and that I had so much to teach her. As for Doug, I didn't want to leave him destitute—emotionally, financially, or organizationally. At various times, these worries seemed so big as to potentially overwhelm me. And there weren't easy answers. I had to work through each crisis point before tackling the next. In many ways, this book exists because I felt so unprepared to leave my loved ones. Working through this checklist gave me the peace I needed to feel I could leave my family and friends. I still become sad at the thought of possibly not seeing Peyton grow up. The difference is that in the past, when I thought about this, I would feel inconsolable. Now, with the checklist completed, I can be sad and still feel at peace with what might come to pass.

• **Fear of leaving unfinished business behind.** Every once in a while, I have become panic-stricken at the thought that I will die before I am ready. Usually these frightening moments occurred when my health suddenly deteriorated and I was in the middle of a project that was important to me. The only way I learned to address this fear, which still rises to the surface occasionally, was to find ways to complete what I was doing or let it go. Either I could divide a project up into small pieces so I could finish one piece at a time and get help in completing the other pieces, or I had to take a deep breath and acknowledge that I wouldn't finish everything. This was not easy to do, but it was imperative for my peace of mind.

• **Fear of no life after death.** Now that was a scary thought. Death would be much more frightening if I thought my time on earth was my one and only shot at existence and that my spirit would disappear into nothingness with my death. When I occasionally thought about this question, it could paralyze me with fear. I have always had a strong belief in God, but what if I was wrong and there was no God or spiritual life after death?

After I nearly died from an infection two years ago, this question became moot for me. As I lay near death in the bubble room at the hospital, I felt the presence of a loving, nurturing God near me. In that moment, I knew that God was present when I was born and would be present when I died. It was so clear to me that what waited for me was an indescribable amount of love. Since then, if this fear ever resurfaces, I remember back to my experience in the hospital room and feel immediately at ease. (I'll go into greater detail about my spiritual inquiry in chapter 7.)

• **Fear of the process of dying.** To resolve my concerns about the process of dying, I did some research, as I mention in chapter 6, "The Mental Preparations for Death." Since I have an illness that has a somewhat predictable path, I asked my doctor how I might actually die. I wanted to know the process of dying so that I would not be surprised and would not worry about it in advance. As it turned out, my doctor's explanation was more descriptive than I had anticipated, but through these conversations I gained a greater sense of control because, with the information, I could choose in advance how I wanted to be treated medically. Ultimately, I found it was helpful to learn exactly what might occur. In addition, after nearly dying, I stopped worrying about the actual moment of death. I had come so close to dying and had felt such peace that I knew, when the time came, the experience of death would be peaceful.

As a terminally ill patient, I made other process-oriented decisions about whether I would stay at home, go to the hospital, or go to hospice for end-of-life care. I thought about how I would say good-bye to Peyton if I were taken to the hospital knowing I might not return home. I talked with Doug about his feelings if I were to die at home. One step at a time, I have looked at each of these fears about the process of dying and put them aside.

➤ Everyone has his or her own particular fears about death. Some other fears or worries I have heard are a:

• Feeling of not having lived a fulfilled life
• Feeling that talents and gifts have not been used
• Fear that death might be painful
• Fear of losing mental or physical capacities
• Fear about what comes after death, if anything
• Sadness at not having time to finish projects or life work
• Sadness at missing a future that won't be experienced

One prominent minister asked his colleagues to tell him the questions they most often hear from people who are confronting death. He gathered together these questions:[3]

• How can I know that I will go to heaven?
• What will heaven be like?
• When will it happen? When will I be with God?
• How can I be certain?
• Who will go to heaven? Who will not?
• If I have been married more than once, who will be my spouse in heaven?

---

3. Reverend Mark Craig, Highland Park United Methodist Church.

- Will I be old or young, in health or in sickness?
- Will my dog go with me?
- Will I see my loved ones again?
- What about those who commit suicide?
- Why eternal life?

Addressing these questions and fears can be hard going. If you do not have someone in your immediate circle who can constructively help you think through your unique fears of death, there are some excellent counselors who specialize in helping people find peace in their lives and with death. To find a counselor, contact your doctor, a local hospice, church, synagogue, or mosque and ask for recommendations.

❏ Know that there is no right way to grieve.

Naturally, Mom and Dad had a particularly difficult time coming to terms with the idea that they might outlive me. Children weren't supposed to die before their parents. My parents had spent a good part of their lives feeling responsible for my well-being; here my life was in jeopardy, and they could not control my fate. Of all the trials for a parent, watching a child die must be the most difficult. Though I have wanted to put myself in my parents' shoes so I would understand what they are experiencing, I cannot fathom going through this with Peyton.

People grieve in different ways, which certainly holds true for parents. When I nearly died and was isolated in a hospital room for three weeks, my mother later told me she hit a wall. The thought of me dying was so totally overwhelming and unacceptable to her that she did not know what to do. Up until then, she had thought she could somehow control the outcome; if she helped find the right specialists, took good enough care of me, prayed hard enough, I would be OK. During those weeks when I was in the hospital and my prognosis was so dire, my mother visited the hospital chapel every day. She talked to God in a way she never had before, and ultimately, she turned my fate over to Him. She absolved herself of feeling responsible for whether I lived or died and shifted her whole being by relying on her faith to carry her through.

Whereas my mother found relief from "anticipatory grief" by turning my fate over to God, my father has continued to believe I will beat the cancer and to pray to God for my healing. Like Mom, Dad has been there for Doug and me throughout. Although their approaches have been different, Mom and Dad have not been in conflict over them. I have come to think that the most important aspect of my parents' handling of my illness has been their deep love and respect for each other. They have supported each other as they have grieved differently in anticipation of my possible death. If I were to pass away first, they would no doubt support each other through that whole new realm of grieving.

Though I can't understand what my parents have gone through over the last four years, we have talked about it together. I raised the issue of their grieving with them because I did not want them to feel they had to manage on their own or hide their feelings to "protect" me. When we talked about how they were feeling and coping, we all grew stronger and closer. My parents were relieved not to have to pretend they were feeling one way when, in actuality, they were feeling another. There still are times when they feel sad and do their best to hide their emotions, but generally, during our good times together—and we've had a lot—we have not felt weighed down by unspoken feelings of remorse and sadness. My parents have been an incredible example for me as I have watched them process their own grief, and in turn, I have learned to process my own.

➤ Grieving involves accepting reality and coming to terms with it, and we each have our own way of handling this difficult process. Grieving can be made even more difficult when loved ones handle and express their grief in different ways. For example, couples who lose a child can find that the grief process puts a terrible strain on their marriage, sometimes causing insurmountable obstacles for the couple. Churches, synagogues, mosques, hospices and other organizations offer excellent grief and recovery counseling and workshops that can be helpful to people who have suffered the loss of a loved one.

❑ **Be sensitive to the changing dynamics within your family or circle of friends.**

It has been four years since my cancer diagnosis—and a long haul for my family and friends who have cared for me. At one point, my siblings worried about our parents, who were giving so much of themselves. Debbi, Noreen, and Michael were concerned that Mom and Dad would become emotionally and physically exhausted over time. My siblings did not know whether to step in and say something to me, particularly given my precarious health. After much soul searching, they decided that sharing their observations would be an expression of their love for our parents and me. My sister Debbi talked with me about my parents' unselfish giving.

In response to her call, Doug and I immediately asked my parents to dinner to discuss the "state of the nation." We learned that when I called my parents for something, they would drop whatever they were doing or cancel whatever plans they had. I, on the other hand, called them all the time, not knowing what a disruption I had become to their lives. The way I looked at it, I called on my favorite people when I needed someone with me. For instance, with my list of baby-sitters for Peyton, I called my favorites first, in hopes that they would be available. Over dinner, I realized what a burden I had become. It took asking them point blank if they had been canceling their plans for me to learn what had been going on. My parents acknowledged that they found it impossible to say "no" to me, given my situation. So, we made a pact. They would try to share their schedules with me, and I would call on friends and others when I needed company for anything other than critical meetings and procedures.

My siblings also voiced their concern that, since I got cancer, most of the major holidays had revolved around me, with their families having to travel to Dallas for our festivities. We just kept thinking that yet again it was my "last" Christmas or Thanksgiving. Actually, this became a bit of a family joke. However, over time, my sisters and brother missed Mom and Dad's involvement in their lives. Since we didn't all live in the same city, it was important for my brother and sisters to feel that Mom and Dad would join some of their families' special occasions. At the time, my parents were surprised by my siblings' comments, in part because they had become so caught up in taking care of me. Once they heard what Debbi, Noreen and Michael had to say, they understood completely, as did I. They have made adjustments to spend more time with them.

> ➤ It is incredibly important for family members and friends to gauge one another's feelings and frustrations, even if all that needs to be said is "We miss you." This particularly holds true for teenage children, who need extra love and attention when someone close to them is ill. Sometimes children are left out of conversations because adults do not have the time to talk with them or think they will not understand. Children do understand a great deal, and they need to be told that their feelings and frustrations are valid and important.

❏ **Be sensitive to the new roles played by your caregivers.**
The roles played by my family members have shifted dramatically since I became ill. Before the cancer, I provided a meaningful income to the family, worked from home so I could keep an eye on Peyton, and managed the household. When my illness set in, Doug took on much more. He became the sole breadwinner, having to cover our regular expenses plus the additional medical and personnel costs, and—during his "off" time—take care of both Peyton and me. In his expanded role, Doug's biggest challenge was time management. Finding the time and energy to balance work, care for me and Peyton, and run the household—not to mention see to his own needs—created a strain.

For my parents, my illness thrust them back into the role of parenting. Just as their four children settled into their own families, Mom and Dad reverted to caring for me. Before I got cancer, they had planned to build their dream house and retire near Austin, Texas. They had sold the family ranch, drawn up blueprints for the house, and even bought the land. After I got sick, they scrapped all the plans and stayed in Dallas to be near me— an incredible sacrifice on their part. Now, instead of enjoying their retirement and having time to travel together, they stay by my side and shuttle me to and from the doctors when Doug is at work. They have repeatedly canceled trips when my health has taken a sudden turn for the worse, and they have organized their lives around my need for care. While I haven't heard them complain, I know they worry about having enough time to spend time just enjoying each other.

My challenge throughout all this has been not to take Doug, Mom, and Dad's time and love for granted. This has been a long haul, and I have had to remind myself and them that they need their own space and time to do other things for themselves.

❏ **Take care of your caregivers.**

When I was in college, my boyfriend of five years was in a serious car accident. Brad went from being a world-class decathlete who was training for the Olympics to being in a coma and, after he regained consciousness, to being partially paralyzed. After the accident, I temporarily left college to be by his bedside and do whatever I could for Brad and his family. I'll never forget how helpless and frustrated I felt. No matter how hard I tried, I could not control the speed or quality of Brad's recovery. Seeing Brad go through lengthy and difficult rehabilitation to relearn fundamental physical and mental processes broke my heart. Brad recovered his health and is happily married, and I learned an important lesson. Since then, I have always believed that managing a serious illness is harder on loved ones than it is on the person being cared for. Since getting cancer, I have often thought back on this experience and have reminded Doug and my parents of it. There is no doubt that the last four years have been a great deal tougher on Doug and my parents than on me. The caregiver often needs more love and support than the patient.

Doug has often said, "This is a marathon, not a sprint." Throughout the progression of my disease, my husband and parents (my "A-Team") have periodically become burned out by the demands of their caregiver roles. We all have had to learn to pace ourselves, which has not been easy. We have learned several things:

1. Define the roles of your caregivers. When a friend learned she had cancer, I wrote her a letter advising her to define the roles of her caregivers. Following is an excerpt of that letter:

When you create your support system, you may wish to think in terms of A, B and C teams:

The A-Team
The A-Team consists of one to four people with whom you are absolutely comfortable and from whom you gain strength. Ask yourself if you would want to face a crisis with these individuals. Would you mind if they saw you throw up? Could you feel open enough to say that you were scared, and know that they would comfort you and not judge you? For me, my A-Team consisted of my husband, mother, and father. All three have been present at the "big" meetings with the oncologist and whenever scans were read. That way, the A-Team members could hear the prognosis first-hand, ask their own questions and discuss the next steps. Sometimes it is difficult to hear everything the doctor says, especially when the news is not good or the doctor asks me to make complicated desicions. With my A-Team by my side, we would all ask different questions and would absorb different pieces of information. When it came to making a decision, we would talk together with the doctor until the facts were in hand and a consensus emerged.

The B-Team

The B-Team is comprised of other family members, close friends, meal preparers and child-care givers—individuals you can rely on to help you manage your household. Your B-Team is particularly important when you feel ill. I recommend asking your doctors and nurses what to expect from different treatments or from the disease itself so you can plan in advance for your B-Team to support you. At these times, you will need groceries purchased, meals prepared, someone to pay the bills and deposit checks, and someone to be with you during the day when you are home. Since your A-Team is so busy assisting you emotionally and physically, try involving the B-Team in helping with these day-to-day needs. If your family or friends are unavailable, you might want to hire someone to help you on those days when you are feeling particularly ill.

The C-Team

Members of this team are family and friends who can help with particular tasks but cannot be relied upon for long engagements. C-Team members can make the occasional meal, accompany you to the hospital when you arrange it in advance, take you to the movies when you feel the urge for a change, etc.

One word of caution: Some potential caregivers might consider moving so they can be nearer to you. For them, it is natural to want to drop everything to help when someone they love is in crisis. My brother, Michael, moved to Dallas so he could be with me and help with my care. At the time, I was under the impression that the main reason he moved back was to join my father's business, and we did not discuss the full ramifications of his move. He now realizes that, in his case, he could have contributed just as effectively without giving up the life that he and his wife, Lisa, had established and loved.

Should someone in your life consider moving near you, talk together about the short- and long-term implications of the move, both to the person individually and to his or her family.

2. Caregivers need permission to take a break and enjoy themselves. My health has sometimes been so precarious that my husband and parents have felt either unwilling or unable to take time to relax. Doug has often felt so guilty about taking time away he hasn't been able to relax and enjoy himself. Another problem has been finding someone to look after me and Peyton if Doug wanted to leave the house. Rather than going through the hassle of finding someone to cover for him, he would stay home. Going out spontaneously was out of the question.

This was a big problem. We all need time to recharge our batteries, to have some fun, to catch up with other people in our lives—and to do so guilt-free. As Doug said, "I can't sustain the speed I'm driving at if I don't re-gas the engine." Most importantly, my A-Team needed to hear from me that I wanted them to enjoy themselves—and that feeling guilty defeated the purpose of relaxing.

3. Caregivers should take breaks even when they don't get your wholehearted approval. When I wasn't feeling well, I've felt torn when Doug, Mom, and Dad wanted to take breaks. Intellectually, I knew they needed time for themselves, but emotionally, I wanted one of them around and felt disappointed or rejected when they went off on their own. Weekends were especially precious because Doug and I would share them with Peyton. When Doug left to go to work or exercise on Saturdays, I would feel disappointed not to have the whole weekend with him. For Doug, working out was essential to his mental and physical well-being.

There have been other times when I have needed Doug's emotional support so much that I ignored his own needs. The analogy that comes to mind is the drowning swimmer whose panic causes her to pull the lifeguard under water with her. There have been numerous times when I have kept Doug awake at night because I was upset about something and wanted to talk with him about it. During these late-night sessions, I knew intellectually that I was wearing him out and that he needed to rest before going to work the next day, but I couldn't stop myself. Sometimes my emotional needs were so strong that I couldn't pull back and think of Doug's interests. These times have been hard on Doug because he finds it almost impossible to say no to me when I need his wisdom, comfort, and support so badly. I am dealing with this better, but I still find myself having to learn to give him the space he needs for himself.

4. Caregivers should check in with you and each other. Doug, Mom, Dad, and I have made a point of having dinner every so often to touch base and catch up with one another. These gatherings have become a chance for us to talk about how things are going, find out how each one of us is holding up under the strain, and make changes to our routine to ease the burden on one another.

5. Caregivers should respect each other's relationship with the ill person. My "A-Team" members have been very careful not to step on one another's toes. For example, my parents have taken on much of my daytime care. They have spent untold hours at home with me when Doug has been at work. It would have been easy for my parents to assume that they could come and go and make themselves totally at home when Doug was there; after all, Mom and Dad were there almost daily when he was gone. They have not done that, though, because it was Doug's and my home. Mom and Dad have been sensitive to the fact that after Doug returns home from work, the household is Doug's and mine to run. It is our family unit, and they are my parents. Thankfully, Mom and Dad have made sure that Doug hasn't felt disenfranchised in his own home.

➤ If you have traveled on a commercial airplane, you've heard the preflight safety instructions: In the event of an emergency and if the plane's cabin loses pressure, adults are instructed to put on their own oxygen masks first, before placing oxygen masks on their children. Though these instructions at first seem counterintuitive, almost selfish, they make sense. If you pass out from lack of oxygen, you can't be much help for your children. The same goes for caregivers. If caregivers don't take care of their basic needs, they won't do a good job of caring.

➤ If you are ill, I suggest making a deliberate effort to gauge the feelings and well-being of the people who shoulder the burden of your care. Talk with them about any changes in the routine that are needed to give them the breaks they need to stay strong and healthy themselves.

➤ There are stories of caregivers physically or emotionally abusing their terminally ill patients. One cause of this abuse might be that the caregivers do not have a moment for themselves. If there is no respite for caregivers—to take a day off or run an errand during the day—they will start to feel angry and frustrated. Everyone needs a break to reestablish his or her own equilibrium.

❏ **Be conscious of people and activities that deplete your energy.**

Positive energy is as critical to everyday happiness as it is to daily healing. When I have felt ill, positive energy has been as important as food and sleep. Some people give me energy, whereas others deplete my energy. Although I have found no hard and fast characteristics of these two types of people, I have made some generalizations. People who have tended to give me positive energy are:

• Sensitive to my physical well-being
• Good listeners
• Willing to just sit with me without talking if I am feeling weak
• Positive in their outlook
• Willing to discuss meaningful, non-cancer-related topics

People who drain my energy are people who:

- Require me to lead the conversation or fill in big conversational gaps
- Want to get the latest detailed overview on my health
- Like to discuss mundane topics
- Cannot modify their own energy levels to fit mine

Certain activities and environments also have a detrimental effect on my energy level. Loud, fast-paced restaurants often tire me out. Mundane activities deplete me. For example, if I spend time on finances, which was my comfort zone as a venture capitalist, I start to feel physically tired. Finance gives me no mental, emotional, or physical sustenance. If I focus on tedious activities, I feel my life energy draining away. At times when I must complete a tiresome task, I first ask someone to help me, and then if I am on my own, I try to get it done as quickly as I can, without making the project bigger than it needs to be.

❏ **Give yourself the emotional leeway to adjust to your physical limitations.**

As I have mentioned, when I first learned I had cancer, I tried to live my life as normally as possible. I did not want to interrupt our family's routines or be a burden to people. In particular, I wanted to stay in control of what was happening to me. When I started the heavy-dose chemotherapy treatments, things changed. I couldn't command my body to do what I wanted. I used to be able to go day and night to complete a project. Before Peyton was born, I routinely went to work at 7:00 A.M. and returned home at 9:30 P.M.—and still had energy. I loved outdoor activities, especially fishing, scuba diving, and river rafting. In contrast, for the last year, I have been unable to drive, shop for myself, or even sit at the kitchen table most nights of the week. With the treatments, I sometimes could barely walk. I got angry and frustrated that my body was letting me down. My mother remembers me saying repeatedly, "This is so dumb. Why can't I get around?" Then I would try to walk (when I should have been in a wheelchair) and would needlessly exhaust myself.

At other times I would be sad when I didn't have the energy to play with Peyton. When I was on heavy medications, her exuberance would tire me out. As a 'type A' personality, dealing with fatigue was particularly frustrating. When I was feeling tired and ill and couldn't go upstairs to tuck Peyton into bed at night, I would feel especially lonely missing out on that special time with Peyton.

Also, since getting ill, both Doug and I have had to adjust to my lack of interest in sex following the intense chemotherapy. Even when I have felt the desire to make love to my husband, my body has been unable to handle it. I've become too weak and fragile to share this with Doug, which has been difficult for both of us. We have tried to compensate for this deficit by cuddling and touching, though even that can be a problem when I am not feeling well. Doug says that getting plenty of exercise has helped to relieve some of the strain.

It took time, but I gradually came to accept each physical limitation. Sharing my feelings with Doug and friends helped ease the intensity of the emotions. Sometimes a good cry would make me feel better. At other times, I just had to give myself leeway to adjust to a new reality before I could let go of the negative emotions. I did not want to dwell on the difficult aspects of being ill or on feeling sorry for myself, so I would try to find ways to still enjoy what I liked doing, even if I couldn't participate fully. For example, Peyton was an enormous priority for me, so I would save up my energy to be with her. I would take it easy during the day so that when she came home from school, I could focus on her. She and I both learned to tone down our activities so I would not get so drained. She would often snuggle with me and tell me about what she had learned in school or her activities that day. We couldn't wrestle on the lawn together, but we could find other new ways to enjoy our time together. I must say, as long as I am alive and can enjoy my family and friends, I consider myself lucky. It's amazing that two years ago, I was unable to move at all and almost died in the bubble room. I have had a very full two years despite my physical limitations.

❑ **Get the support you need to adjust to changes in your physical appearance.**

According to my nurse, the most challenging and emotional issue her patients faced was the deterioration of their bodies. Weight loss, in particular, was difficult to handle. I've been no different. My weight loss over time has felt like a physical manifestation of the possibility of a slow death. To look at my legs and see my femur through the skin and the lack of muscle mass in my calves has been disheartening. Under the supervision of my physician, I have used numerous techniques to try to bulk up, such as drinking soy protein shakes, pureeing my food for easy digestion, and even receiving food intravenously when I have needed it.

Hair loss has been another hurdle. After four years of on-again, off-again chemotherapy, I have lost my hair so many times, it barely fazes me now. The first few times it happened, though, were hard. I went from having lots of long hair to a *GI Jane*–Demi Moore look—without the body to balance the baldness. Socially, my sudden hair loss felt like a statement of illness, a reflection of my loss of control. In addition, I worried about being physically attractive to my husband. Doug was a great help as I got used to the new me. To this day, he says he thinks I am beautiful bald. But then again, he also thought I was pretty when I was pregnant. It took a while for me to believe him, but Doug says he sees my beauty by looking in my eyes. He looks for the soul, and not the outward appearance. The hardest thing for him was when my eyelashes fell off, because they changed the look of my eyes.

❑ **Create short-term goals for yourself.**

On the few occasions since getting cancer when I have not had short-term goals for myself, I have been terrified. Without something to engage my heart and mind, all I have focused on is my body and its gradual deterioration. I have needed a reason to live and sustain myself. When I had a project or task that I was excited about completing, that energy seemed to balance the negative energy emanating from my body when I was ill. Those positive sentiments actually made me feel healthier and stronger. The trick was finding goals that really meant something to me— not just things that needed to get done, but something I cared deeply about completing or participating in—like working on this checklist. Sometimes, when I completed a goal, I have asked my family members and friends to help me think of a new one.

IF YOU ARE A PARENT OR GRANDPARENT

❑ **Do not tell a young child a specific time frame when a parent might die, unless death is imminent.**

Thank goodness my doctors have been better at keeping me alive than estimating my life expectancy! Over the last four years, we have "lived through" several predictions of my premature demise. Every time we heard a negative prognosis and corresponding time frame, our hearts would sink. Then I'd live past the milestone, only to hear the next. Although we encouraged our doctors to give us their best guess on my prognosis, it was sometimes difficult to keep our hopes and energies focused on a positive outcome when the news was bad. We decided early on that we would not subject Peyton to this rollercoaster ride. Our approach has been to say to Peyton, "Mom could die from cancer; however, only God knows when I will die." Peyton knows that God could decide to take one of us, and no one knows when that might be. We have emphasized that God loves us and her. In a concerted effort not to transfer our concerns to Peyton, we have avoided sharing with her the constant ups and downs of my prognosis.

> ➤ I do not believe in giving young children a specific time frame for when a parent or grandparent may die, particularly if the ill person is months away from possibly dying. However, if the death of a parent or grandparent is a few weeks away, parents can prepare their young children with

more definitive language, all the while giving the children a chance to express themselves.

➤ If your children are teenagers, you might choose to share everything you know with them, depending on their emotional maturity and stability. Since teenagers can be very good at sizing up a situation, it might be easier on them to be told what is happening than to be left in the dark. If they know there's a problem, their imagination could make things worse than they actually are. Still, based on the reality of the situation I recommend being as upbeat as possible. With Peyton I have said that I would be with God looking over her. Before talking with your teenage children, you might ask a psychological counselor for advice on how best to talk about your health and life expectancy with them.

❏ **Tell your children how much you love them.**

I have known people who, as they lay dying, did not want to fully express their love for their children, for fear that their children would then miss them even more after their parent passed away. This "protective mechanism" is terribly misguided. Children flourish when they know they are loved. We all do. While it is extremely sad for someone to lose a loved one, it is even sadder for that love to be held in reserve. Researchers have done all sorts of tests that prove children and adults live happier, healthier lives if they felt loved when they were young.

One of my goals after I got cancer was to live to see Peyton's fifth birthday. I knew that the first five years of life were the most important to a child's development, and I wanted to make sure that, in those five years, I instilled in her a deep-seated belief in my love for her. I lived to see her fifth birthday, and her sixth, and have taken great pleasure in expressing my love to her and receiving hers in return. In my heart, I am confident she will go through life feeling secure in the love there is for her in the world.

I must add that sharing my love with Peyton—and with everyone I love—has had a profound effect on me. When I reached out and loved them, they loved me right back. The energy and warmth that came from that love was so incredibly life-affirming, I don't know how I would have lived without it. In fact, I'm certain I wouldn't have. One of the reasons I have beaten the odds and have lived this long—I am convinced—is, I have been surrounded by love.

➤ Let your children know how much you love them. They can never feel too much love. Think of your love as a gift for their lifetime. Hold and comfort them, and listen to what's on their minds, all the while maintaining your household standards of behavior and discipline. They will learn from you how to love, and then they will love others in turn. And, in the meantime, you will live a longer, healthier life because the love being shared will help sustain you.

➤ It is equally important for others in the family to shower the children with love, especially at a time when the children might lose a parent or grandparent. I have seen families become so overwhelmed by the imminent death of a loved one that they have ignored the interests and needs of the children. I encourage remaining family members to love and support the children through this difficult time. For Doug, faced with the possibility of becoming a single parent, having his own loving and communicative relationship with Peyton has been an enormous priority. They do have that, which has been an great comfort to me.

❑ **Create continuity for your children, should you die.**

Peyton flourished when she had structure, consistency, and continuity in her life. Like most young children, when forced out of her daily routines, Peyton would become irritable and frustrated. After I was diagnosed with cancer, we found the impromptu demands of my illness and the treatments wreaked havoc on Peyton's schedule. Doug and I decided we needed to add continuity and routine back into her life.

Before cancer, Doug and I shared the responsibilities of putting Peyton to bed and getting her up in the morning. Once my cancer treatments started and my health became erratic, I just couldn't count on participating in these rituals every day. So, we decided Doug should take over the nighttime and morning routines with Peyton. Without telling Peyton why, Doug started putting Peyton to bed and getting her up in the morning. This took some adjusting for me. At first, I felt terribly left out. When I heard Peyton and Doug giggling and playing upstairs before bedtime, I had to remind myself not to feel sad. It had been our decision to encourage Doug to take over this responsibility because I had difficulty going upstairs, and I knew it was the right decision, even if I sometimes felt lonely. I had lots of other time during the afternoons to play with Peyton.

It wasn't long before Peyton and Doug established their own bedtime routines, playing catch with a Nerf football, brushing her teeth, reading a book and saying prayers around a lit prayer candle. For the first time, Doug and Peyton had scheduled time together for just the two of them, and it was great for their relationship. Peyton and I continued to spend lots of time together during the day, so I got over the feeling of missing out on something. Besides, when I have felt physically strong enough, I have sometimes made it upstairs to join them at bedtime. Now I know, if I die soon, two very important rituals of Peyton's— going to bed and getting up in the morning—will remain intact. At least in these two areas, Peyton would not feel a terrible break in her daily routine.

Continuity also figured into our choice of schools for Peyton. Peyton attended an exceptional school for children in pre-kindergarten and kindergarten. Within two years, Peyton would have had to leave this school to enter first grade. Her new school offered classes for students in kindergarten through grade twelve. The question was: Should we move Peyton a year early so her mother could help with the transition? What if I died before Peyton entered first grade, and Peyton had to deal with both her mother's death and a new school? We decided to transfer Peyton to the new school a year early. Although it now looks as if I will live to see Peyton enter first grade, by making the early transition, I have had a chance to meet and get to know the staff, the administration, the parents, and the other students in the school Peyton may attend for many years. Peyton is fully acclimated and loves her new academic surroundings, something which gives me great peace of mind.

❏ **Hire a full-time caregiver for your children.**

(Note: For additional considerations on hiring a caregiver, see pages 142–145.)

When we realized I might die from this disease, I would often wake up in the middle of the night worrying about Peyton's future care. It was upsetting to think of her growing up without a mother, and Doug and Peyton having to manage on their own. I was especially troubled by thinking about how difficult things might be for them immediately after my death. I reached a point where I had to do something.

At the same time, Doug worried about juggling Peyton's needs with the demands of work and the household, if I were to pass away. The demands of taking care of me, Peyton, his job, house chores, and meals were already taking a toll on him. Often he felt torn between handling his work responsibilities, his daughter's upbringing, and my care.

After several long discussions, we decided to hire a full-time caregiver for Peyton, someone who was loving and trustworthy and who would become a part of our household while I was still alive. That person would not take on my role; instead, she would supplement it. She could help in managing Peyton's schedule, playing with her when I wasn't physically strong enough to do so, and organizing our household. The more we thought about this, the more certain we were that it was the right approach. By finding a caregiver early on, we both saw some important benefits.

1. Doug and I could handpick the person together. We felt certain we had a better chance of selecting the right per-

son if we worked together. Also, by talking about the pros and cons of each candidate, we could develop and make priorities for the qualities we wanted in the caregiver.

2. Without my input, Doug thought finding a caregiver after my possible death would be a nightmare.

3. Peyton could get used to the caregiver's presence, see her as an integral part of our household, and come to love and trust her.

4. The caregiver could learn the morals, values, and routines I wished to instill in Peyton. (I have worked with my daughter's caregiver to share my approach to developing Peyton's self-esteem, disciplining her, following our household routines, praying, arranging after-school activities, etc.)

5. If my health declined or I passed away, Doug would have the support of someone he knew and trusted to help in taking care of Peyton and the household.

6. If I had a remission or recovered from the illness, I could rely on the caregiver to reduce stress and increase the time available to me for healing and rest.

7. If the caregiver did not work out, we had time to find another person.

I cannot overemphasize how important hiring a caregiver was for me. I have seen several friends die of breast cancer. At the ends of their lives, they were panic-stricken about leaving their children behind without a plan for their care.

Before hiring a caregiver, so many of our late-night worries had to do with the logistics of taking care of Peyton and allowing for continuity and routine in her life. These anxieties have disappeared. Doug feels confident with our arrangements. I know that my death, if it comes with this disease, will be hard on Peyton, but at least the people and systems are in place to give her the support and love she will need.

➤ If you are a parent of children under the age of eighteen, I recommend identifying, interviewing, and *hiring* the next caregiver for your children (assuming the remaining parent will have to work or will not be available to welcome the children home from school). Continuity and routine are critical to children, who want to know, "Who will take care of me if you die?" It is extremely important for children to receive full-time, consistent care after a parent dies. Now is not the time to pass the children between neighbors and other caregivers, but to make sure the children can depend upon a solid, responsible person for their care. The support of a strong and reliable caregiver can greatly contribute to the emotional well-being of the entire household.

➤ If your family or friends are pitching in to help care for your children while you are alive, it is important to talk with them about the care they can commit to in the event of your death. If the people you choose to care for your children feel unable to handle the responsibility for the long term, find full-time caregiving for your children now. Otherwise, your children will suffer from the disruption in care.

❑ **Let important people in your children's lives know how you are doing.**

Over the years, we found that rumors about my health and well-being would get started among Peyton's school friends and their parents. Since we thought this misinformation was potentially damaging for Peyton and her classmates, we decided to keep the school community updated on my progress and the approach we were taking with Peyton. To that end, we wrote occasional letters to the administrators, teachers, and parents at Peyton's school explaining the latest news on my health, how we were talking with Peyton about it, and our hopes that they would be particularly sensitive when talking with Peyton about my health.

In addition to our letters, we have visited Peyton's teachers to talk about her development and to learn if she was adjusting well or had displayed any behavioral problems that might have been attributed to worries about me. If Peyton's behavior or conversations changed in any significant way, either in the classroom or on the playground, we wanted to know about it. In all, we took great comfort in knowing her teachers were united with us in looking after Peyton's welfare.

> ➤ Write a letter to the parents of your children's classmates and the school administrators, letting them know how you are doing physically and how you would like them to interact with your children regarding your illness. Thank them for their concern, and ask them to call you if any questions come up or if they want to talk with you for any reason.

❏ **Talk with your family and friends about the children-to-children dynamic.**

When Peyton was five, my sister took her to the State Fair. In the backseat of the car, Peyton said to her cousin, Evan, who was two years old, that some day her mommy or daddy may die and go to heaven, but we don't know when. Peyton wasn't worried or anxious. She was calmly explaining to her much younger cousin what she had heard from us. Evan, who had never heard such talk, became scared. It did not take long for my sister to explain things to her son so he no longer felt afraid, but it did raise an issue. Our family and close friends needed to coordinate our conversations about life and death and about the state of my health. That way, the parents could have the appropriate conversations with their children, and we could let Peyton know which of her cousins and friends were too young to have such conversations.

> ➤ Ask your extended family and close family friends if they have talked with their children about the concept of death and dying. Share with them the approach you have taken with your children, and ask if they would consider hold-

ing similar conversations with their children so that the cousins and young friends do not inadvertently confuse or frighten each other. Also, tell your children who in the family is too young to talk with about this.

❏ **Interview and select counselors for your children in case they need counseling.**

Should I die, Peyton might need to talk with a counselor to get assistance in grieving. With so many counselors to choose from, it was difficult for Doug and me to know who was qualified and reputable. Our approach was to research and interview a number of counselors. Among other things, we asked them to tell us how they would help a child grieve. What a horrifying range of answers we received! Without taking into consideration our own thoughts, many counselors would have talked to Peyton about concepts that were completely inconsistent with her upbringing and the conversations we had already had with her about the concept of death. One counselor, in particular, said that she would suggest that Peyton climb into an empty casket to get a feeling of closure with my death—something we thought was a terrible idea! We were not impressed by a number of people in this field. At a particularly vulnerable point in her life, Peyton could have been subjected to some confusing and harmful approaches. Eventually, we found an excellent counselor who could be an excellent resource for Peyton should she need one.

➤ In the event of your passing, many counselors will be available to your children to assist them with their grief. **Be cautious** when selecting a counselor. Children's minds are very delicate at this time and can be easily influenced. We recommend that you and your spouse interview possible counselors ahead of time. That way, if your child seeks counseling, his or her experiences with the counselor will be positive and helpful.

❑ **Let your family members and close friends know how you would like them to interact with your children, should you pass away suddenly.**

I created a list of my friends and family members and their various strengths, with the recommendation that Peyton and Doug might turn to them for advice or insight. For example, one friend is good at articulating her thoughts and could help Peyton and Doug think through how they might position a new idea or concept. Another friend was good at organizing events and activities. I suggested people they could turn to for spiritual counsel and, for Peyton, advice on boys or advice when she is having trouble communicating with her father. For Doug, I recommended whom he might turn to for information on the school system (such as which teachers had the strongest teaching skills) and parents who knew which extracurricular activities were the most enriching for children.

❑ **If you believe in God, talk to your children about their relationship with God.**

In the spiritual section, I recommend praying with your children. I bring it up again here because I have found that prayer can be soothing to the emotions of children (not to mention my own!). Doug, Peyton, and I often have prayed together, taking turns talking aloud to God, telling Him what we were thankful for, and asking for His blessings. During these prayers, we have been surprised by what Peyton said and amazed at her ability, at a very young age, to create her own unique understanding with God. After these prayers together, we all have felt immensely more peaceful and united as a family.

Prayer is part of Doug's nighttime ritual with Peyton. Sometimes they say prayers around a lit prayer candle and other times they say prayers from Peyton's bed. Doug leads off by saying a new prayer each night in which he recounts his blessings and spiritual thoughts. Then he encourages her to pray from the heart. In the process, Peyton learns to articulate her spirituality, and Doug has the opportunity to hear what Peyton is thankful for each day. I'm not sure who enjoys their prayer time more, Doug or Peyton!

CHAPTER SUMMARY

❏ Notify loved ones of your illness.
❏ Allow yourself to be pleasantly surprised by the people in your life.
❏ Learn how to receive from friends and strangers.
❏ Let people know how they can help you.
❏ Communicate with your loved ones.
❏ Reach your own peace with your illness.
❏ Create a strategy for treating your illness.
❏ Address your fears about death.
❏ Know that there is no right way to grieve.
❏ Be sensitive to the changing dynamics within your family or circle of friends.
❏ Be sensitive to the new roles played by your caregivers.
❏ Take care of your caregivers.
❏ Be conscious of people and activities that deplete your energy.
❏ Give yourself the emotional leeway to adjust to your physical limitations.
❏ Get the support you need to adjust to changes in your physical appearance.
❏ Create short-term goals for yourself.

If You Are a Parent or Grandparent
❏ Do not tell a young child a specific time frame when a parent might die, unless death is imminent.
❏ Tell your children how much you love them.
❏ Create continuity for your children, should you die.
❏ Hire a full-time caregiver for your children.

❑ Let important people in your children's life know how you are doing.

❑ Talk with your family and friends about the children-to-children dynamic.

❑ Interview and select counselors for your children should they need counseling.

❑ Let your family members and close friends know how you would like them to interact with your children, should you pass away suddenly.

❑ If you believe in God, talk to your children about their relationship with God.

5

THE PHYSICAL PREPARATION FOR DEATH: AN UNSELFISH ACT

~ع چ~

Since we started writing this book, my two coauthors, my husband, Doug, and my close friend, Emily, have lost several loved ones. As I mentioned earlier, Doug's mother passed away, and Emily lost two family members—all in a sixteen-week period. At the time, we were all stunned by the sense of loss. We were also quick to notice that only one of the three had made substantial plans for death. Emily's mother-in-law, Esther Cooper, who had contributed to an early manuscript of this book, shared her wishes with her family before she died. She chose to be cremated and selected the urn (a piece of pottery from her collection of North Carolina pottery). She had loved music her whole life and created a list of her favorite songs to be played and sung at her memorial service. In advance, she articulated her wishes for medical treatment. For her, that meant no extreme measures if death was imminent. With her niece's help, she recorded audiotapes with stories about her life and her sons' early years. These tapes will be played for her future grandchildren in years to come. Following her death, Emily's family took comfort in her mother-in-law's preparations—and in knowing they were adhering to her wishes. While the sadness was tremendous, the family felt relieved she had been so thoughtful as to plan ahead and ease the burden on them.

Some people might think being busy is a good distraction immediately after a loved one dies. We think otherwise. Doug, his father, and his brother would have preferred to spend time together, sharing thoughts and memories of his mother, rather than having to manage the myriad of details associated with planning her funeral service. With all the work that needed to be done, there wasn't much time for them to grieve, separately or together.

If you have not had to manage the arrangements after a loved one has died, it might be difficult to understand the ordeal involved. It can be painful, confusing, and emotionally draining to find oneself in the position of completing someone else's checklist. Seeing how difficult this could be was a powerful motivator for me to face my own apprehensions about the practical aspects of dying. Yes, it was difficult to make arrangements for my own eventual death, but we all will die sometime. When I die, something must be done with my body. My family and friends will want a memorial service so they can share their grief and their memories. Ultimately, preparing for my death was not so much for my own benefit as for that of my loved ones. I have come to believe that being physically prepared for death is one of the most unselfish things a person can do for others. As a side benefit, once the planning is in place, there is the peace and comfort of knowing the burden is lifted for your family and friends.

When Doug and I created this chapter of the checklist, we realized something that now seems obvious: it was vastly easier to tackle the practical items on the list at our leisure and on our own time than immediately following someone's death. As we went through the items on the list and made our end-of-life decisions together, we shared our thoughts and feelings and even found ourselves laughing at the humor that bubbled to the surface as we planned. We completed these plans relatively quickly, limiting the process to only a few meetings and phone calls with service providers. Then, with the preparations behind us, we went on with our lives, knowing that everything was in place should one of us pass away.

➤ By planning your funeral or memorial and your burial or cremation in advance, you can substantially reduce the expenses associated with your burial or cremation. More important, making these decisions greatly eases the emotional burden on your family and friends who otherwise would have to manage the myriad of details at one of the hardest times in their lives.

❏ **Decide if you will be buried or cremated.**

At first, I wanted to be cremated and have my ashes spread across the Caribbean. However, Doug asked me to reconsider. He wanted me to be buried in a conventional gravesite so that he and Peyton could visit my grave together if I died of this disease. When I thought about this decision, I realized I didn't feel strongly about it. Being buried or cremated did not really matter to me. Since Doug did care, I agreed to be buried when I die.

➤ Choose if you will be buried or cremated, and let your family know verbally and in writing of your wishes. Sometimes, you might learn something from the reaction of your loved ones, as I did. Even more importantly, you don't want your family members arguing over the options should you pass away without having decided for yourself.

➤ *Note:* Should you decide to be cremated, on a state-by-state basis, there are membership organizations that offer discounted cremations if you become a member before you die. These associations can offer significant cost savings for people who think ahead.

❏ **Select a cemetery.**

Doug and I agreed that our three most important criteria for evaluating cemeteries in our area were (1) ambiance, (2) proximity, and (3) price. Doug received information on three funeral homes and found their costs to be comparable. What he didn't expect was the magnitude of the costs. Dying wasn't cheap! Here are some of the prices we were quoted.

ITEM	PRICE RANGE
Burial plots	$1,000–$8,500
Caskets	$2,000–$8,000
Headstones	$600–$10,000

After evaluating each cemetery according to our three criteria, we chose a fairly secluded, wooded cemetery about ten minutes from our house.

❏ Make burial arrangements.

Doug likens planning a funeral to planning a vacation. One interacts with the funeral home staff in much the same way as with a travel agent. Both are needed to get you to your destination. The major difference is that, with one, you never want the trip to end, and with the other, you never want the trip to start!

When it came to meeting the funeral home representative to discuss specific gravesite options, plot costs, and other details, I did not want to get directly involved in the discussions. Although I wanted to complete this part of the checklist, I didn't have the emotional or physical energy to manage the details myself. I enlisted my friend, Greg Morgan, to do an initial survey of the various funeral homes. He prepared a matrix with the economics of each option clearly laid out. (As a side note, shortly after Greg completed his research, a dear friend of his passed away, giving him an immediate reason to use the information. While he had gathered the information as a favor to me, it ended up being a resource to him when he needed it.)

With Greg's findings in hand, Doug took over handling the bulk of the arrangements, and I consulted with him in the background. At first, Doug found it hard to get accustomed to the idea of making our burial arrangements. He believed our positive attitudes and visualization could help me stay strong and healthy and worried that finalizing these arrangements could seal my fate. After we talked about this issue, he came to see that no matter when I died, we would both need burial plots. We could make this decision together, as a couple, or one of us would face the decisions alone at some point in the future. Doug did not want to be left to handle this on his own, and besides, he saw it as a family decision. The best thing to do was to get the decision out of the way.

When Doug met with the funeral home sales representative to review the basic offerings, he realized there were more options than he had expected. The sales rep wanted to know if Doug was interested in cremation, above-ground mausoleums, below-ground mausoleums, or standard-ground burial sites. Doug indicated our interest in ground burial sites. With a map of available burial sites in hand, Doug toured the cemetery on his own to get a feel for the various locations. He got out of the car and sat on the benches located near the grave sites to see how it would feel for him to sit with our daughter near my burial site, should I pass away before they do. After selecting his three favorite sites, he came home to discuss the burial options and sites with me. He then chose a beautiful sunny day to drive me through the cemetery to look at the plots. We made the final site selection together, away from any hassles or pressures from the funeral home sales staff. On that visit, we also toured the cemetery, looking at headstones styles and inscriptions, to get a sense of what we wanted.

The next weekend, Doug met with the sales rep and negotiated prices for the burial sites, caskets, interments, burial container, and gravestones we each wanted. Because we had planned in advance, Doug found he could approach the negotiations without emotion, as he would a business deal. As a result, he managed to get a sizable discount on the price of burial packages.

Doug's conversations with the funeral home staff reinforced our belief that planning ahead is the best policy. According to the funeral home staff, an overwhelming number of people wait until someone dies to make funeral arrangements. They commented on how traumatic it was for the deceased's loved ones to make immediate, sensitive, detailed, and costly funeral arrangements during their time of grief and mourning. The staff said that family members have a particularly hard time when the deceased have given no indication of their preferences.

➤ When making your funeral arrangements, I recommend (1) visiting each facility; (2) placing comparable options on an easy-to-read matrix with cost comparisons; and (3) discussing your preferences with your loved ones. Take time to explain to your loved ones that you feel it is important to make these plans so that when you die (hopefully, well in the future) your family and friends will not have to make these decisions and arrangements for you. Once you have made your decisions, negotiate with the funeral home of your choice. As I mentioned earlier, you can negotiate in advance the costs associated with this decision.

➤ If you do not feel up to making your own funeral arrangements, I recommend asking someone to help. That person should have good analytical, financial, and negotiating skills and should follow steps (1) and (2) and then meet with you to review the options. Once you have decided your preferences, your designated person can work with the funeral home to get the best price for you.

❑ **Select your headstone and draft the inscription.**

Doug and I decided to draft our headstone inscriptions because Doug felt it would be difficult to find the appropriate words without knowing my wishes. Once he articulated his feelings, I realized I would have the same problem coming up with his inscription if I did not have his input. Drafting the headstone inscription was surprisingly difficult. Take a moment right now and see what comes to mind for your own inscription. Using only a few words to summarize one's life is a challenge.

In one of the funnier moments during this process, we thought about creating websites and simply listing the Internet addresses on our tombstones. With ErinKramp.rip and DouglasKramp.rip, we could say all we wanted about our lives and our love for the people we left behind. Not to mention, we could include photos, life histories, favorite charities, and other equally fascinating and useful information. (We have yet to act on this idea, however!)

> ➤ As I mentioned in the previous checklist item, advance planning can pay off. Some cemeteries offer headstones at a significant discount if ordered even six weeks in advance.

❏ Decide on an open or closed casket.

Before she died, Doug's mother made it clear that she wanted a closed casket so that her family and friends' last visual memory would be of her alive. Upon her death, it was a relief for Doug to know his mother's wishes.

If you are a parent of young children, I don't recommend an open casket, though there are theories supporting either choice. After contacting adults whose parents had passed away when they were young, every one of them said a closed casket was preferable. Those who had memories of an open casket were disturbed by viewing their dead parent. For some, their last view of their parent in the casket overshadowed their fond memories of them together. This is, however, an age-appropriate issue. For some teenagers, they might need an open casket to bring closure.

A friend, whose mother died when she was young, wrote

I did not see my mother's open casket and to this day I am thankful. The last memory I have of her is of her smiling at me—not dead. However, I did struggle for a while believing that she was dead. For years I wondered if she was really alive and would one day come back—I even looked for her in crowds of people. I really don't know if seeing her body would've added closure or not.

❏ **Consider ways to minimize funeral costs.**

According to the local memorial society, there are some easy ways to minimize funeral costs that you might want to consider. Among their suggestions were:[4]

• **Plan ahead.** Decide what type of arrangements you want. Record these decisions in writing. File them with the funeral home of your choice. You need not pay in advance to file your instructions.

• **Consider type of disposition.** Burial is usually the most expensive option. Cremation costs substantially less. Body donation for medical instruction is the least expensive of all. Remember, cost is one consideration, but not the only one. You need to choose what you and your survivors are comfortable with.

• **Consider separating disposition of the body from the funeral or memorial service.** The funeral service is a necessary ritual to help the survivors accept your death, pay honor to your life, and prepare to face life without you. But all of this can be done without the body present. Services without the body present, often called memorial services, can be just as satisfying and eliminate the pressure of time and other constraints which occur when physical disposition is pending.

• **Consider immediate disposition.** Immediate disposition, by either burial or cremation, eliminates the costs of temporarily preserving the body. It eliminates the need for an elaborate (and expensive) casket to display the dead body. This precludes the practice of viewing the body (which some find distasteful). While the funeral industry promotes viewing on the premise

---

4. Reprinted in part from *Steps to Lower Funeral Costs*, written by the Memorial Service of North Texas, Inc.

that it helps accept the reality of death, this is arguable. It may in fact be a denial of death, pretending it is something else. Viewing would not be popular, and would be unacceptable to the general public, if the body were not treated cosmetically to appear still "lifelike."

• **Consider alternatives to the pre-paid funeral plan.** Totten trusts, dedicated savings plans and dedicated life insurance policies are all ways to provide for funeral costs. They are more flexible.

• **Consider casket alternatives.** Caskets can serve two purposes: (1) as a setting for display of the body during the funeral service and visitation; and (2) as a container for final burial. If you do not choose viewing or a ceremony with the body present, an alternative container, costing about $125, can be used for disposal. Also, rental caskets for the first purpose allows substitution of the less expensive alternative container for the disposal. Many funeral homes now offer rental caskets at savings of as much as 70 percent over purchase.

You do not have to buy the casket from the funeral home that handles the funeral. You can build your own or have one built by a cabinetmaker. You can buy a casket from an independent casket seller. You can even buy it from a different funeral home, one that has lower prices for the model you want.

• **Skip the limousine.** If your service includes accompanying the body to the place of disposition, the funeral home will provide the transportation—at a price. Instead, have family members or friends provide transportation. Arranging and coordinating the transportation can be a way for a family member to participate actively in the service. By the time you have a family car, pallbearers' car, minister's car, lead car, it adds up. If you skip a procession to the place of the disposition, you can eliminate the cost of a motorcycle escort. And ask why a flower car is necessary. Do you really need and want this service?

• **If you are choosing burial, consider purchasing your cemetery plot ahead of time from an individual owner**

rather than the cemetery. There are owners who have changed their plans and so are trying to sell their cemetery plots. Usually they will ask a price lower than plots currently being sold by the cemetery. These often may be in more desirable locations. Check the classified pages of your newspaper.

• **If you are faced with planning a funeral, take a trusted friend along.** You are an amateur buyer of funeral services; funeral directors are professional sellers. Naturally they will try to sell the services that give them the greatest markup. Any sale that entails significant discretionary elements is a power play (at least to some degree) by the seller. Your attorney, financial advisor, minister, or close friend will help even up the power relationship and help you avoid committing for items you do not really want or need.

❑ **Make out-of-state funeral arrangements, if appropriate.**

If you are receiving medical treatments out of state, arrange with a funeral home in the state where you are being treated to be embalmed or cremated before your body is transported across state lines. If this is not arranged in advance, transporting the body after death can be expensive. Do not, however, pre-pay the out-of-state funeral home. Should you die in your home state, the money will be wasted. Again, I recommend asking someone else to handle these arrangements, if at all possible.

❑ **Decide who will write the eulogy.**

Doug decided to write my eulogy. His reasoning was twofold: (1) nobody knew me better than he did, so it was up to him to write it; and (2) there was no way he'd have the emotional bandwidth to express his thoughts and feelings adequately if he waited until after I died. When Doug told me what he planned to do, my reaction was to think, "Isn't this going a bit far?" and "Wow, he must really think I'm going to die." Then, I laughed and realized, well, of course I'll die. Maybe the cause will be this disease and maybe it will be old age. In either case, if writing the eulogy helped Doug prepare, it was fine with me. I just didn't want to hear anything about myself in the past tense.

Doug worked on the eulogy over a period of several weeks, putting it down for a while and then going back to it to add more thoughts. Although he had a difficult time getting started, he ended up getting immersed in the project. He wrote everything in the present tense so he could enjoy thinking about it. Afterward, he said to me that writing the eulogy was the first time he had fully articulated what made me special to him, our family, and friends. At one point, when Doug was out of town, he called me late at night, excited to share a new insight. By then my curiosity about what he was writing was piquing me. It was fun to hear he had discovered new qualities about me that he had taken for granted or not noticed before. That section was the only part of the eulogy he read to me (using the present tense, of course). Once he had written the eulogy, it was easy for him to rewrite it in the past tense so someone could read it on his behalf if he did not feel up to giving it himself.

After he wrote the eulogy, I noticed our communication became stronger and more intimate, which I think was due in part to this exercise. Doug has since asked me to write his eulogy so that I could gain similar insights into him.

➤ Asking someone to write your eulogy might make you uncomfortable if you are strong and healthy, I know. It's one thing if there is a real possibility you might die soon, but what if you live for years and years? What if, as you age, your friendships and allegiances shift so that someone else becomes a better choice to give your eulogy? My recommendation is to view this checklist item as an opportunity to think about and articulate the reasons you care for the person closest to you. Talk to that person about what is to be gained by sharing in the exercise. All of us tend to assume that our family and friends know how much we love them, but seldom do we say directly why we find them to be so remarkable and important to us. Doing so is a precious gift, and there is no time like the present to give it. If, in years to come, your feelings toward the person shift for some reason, you will always have the memory of having shared this exceptional and loving exercise.

➤ If asking someone to write a eulogy seems too hard, consider asking for a "narrative card," which is what Doug gave me several years ago. Doug wrote down why he loved me and what he thought were my special traits. He then read the narrative card to me on my birthday. It was unequivocally the most beautiful card I have ever received. Doug later told me he had referred back to the narrative card when he wrote my eulogy. Many of the points he made in the eulogy came from the card he had written years before. Of course, one doesn't have to wait until a person's birthday to write a narrative card. Any occasion will do. Or no occasion.

❏ **Plan the service.**

As I mentioned earlier, Doug's mother died this year without having made plans for her service. Hours after her death, Doug, his dad and his brother shouldered the responsibility of planning her funeral service. In the midst of all the heartache, Doug wished he knew the passages she wanted read, the songs she wanted sung, and the prayers said. He had no idea what kind of funeral service his mother would have liked. To make matters worse, the pastor at his parents' church did not know his mother very well as she had been bedridden for some time. Within only a few days, they planned his mother's funeral service—and hoped that it reflected her wishes.

Doug and I have made sure our families will not have to go through what he did. We have chosen the format for our services, selected the people we would ask to speak, including the pastor and possible singers (should they agree to participate at the time), and chosen prayers to be read, songs to be sung, and flowers displayed. In addition, we have thought about extra touches we hope will make our services feel warm and personal. For example, we will have a sign-in book for guests and will set aside time during the service for people to stand up and share whatever is on their minds. In addition, we plan to have a book for letters to the family, should people prefer writing their thoughts to speaking publicly.

Doug and I were actually surprised by what we each wanted in our services. There was simply no way he would have guessed the format and content I wanted, or vice versa. Now that we created services that are "ours," our family will have one less thing to think about at "crunch time."

➤ To get started, you might visit a library or bookstore and look over books that offer suggestions for music, prayers and sayings.

➤ If you want a religious service, contact a church, synagogue, or mosque (or other religious institution as suits you) to get copies of programs for funeral or memorial services they have performed in the past. The staff members at these religious institutions are happy to help, and their programs can give you useful ideas on structuring your own service.

❑ **Draft your obituary; choose a black-and-white photograph.**

Again, because I was ill, I did not feel up to writing my own obituary. I gave my father, who was formerly in public relations, my résumé, which he used to write my obituary. In addition, I assembled a list of publications to receive my obituary. Included on the list were my local newspaper, the alumni bulletins from my secondary school and college, and the publications of industry trade associations of which I was a member.

➤ Assembling the facts of your life is a relatively easy task . . . for you. For other people to remember the exact dates and events of your lifetime is surprisingly difficult. Create a record of what you believe are the most significant events and accomplishments of your life.

➤ Some newspapers include more lengthy obituaries on people who have made important contributions during their lives. Other papers accept longer obituaries as advertising and charge a fee to the estate of the deceased. If you think your paper would publish a more detailed obituary on you, create a brief list of people whom the obituary reporter could contact for additional detail on your life.

➤ In addition to selecting the publications to receive your obituary, you might consider designating a charity to receive donations in your name following your death. It has become quite common for people to choose a charity, hospital, or school to receive donations. One way of stating your wishes is to write the last line of your obituary as follows: "In lieu of flowers, the family respectfully requests that donations be made in the name of (your name) to (name of charity and address)." Following your death, the executor of the estate will receive a list of the names of people who contributed in your name. For many families, this tribute to their loved one creates a feeling of community and shared grief that can be very comforting.

❏ **Make these additional decisions about your funeral or memorial and your burial or cremation.**
- Clothing for the deceased
- Vault or crypt
- Type of religious, fraternal, or military service
- Special religious services
- Scripture to be read
- Clergy
- Location of service
- Flowers and music
- Names of pallbearers
- Funeral limousine list
- Special wishes included in the will

IF YOU ARE LIVING WITH A SERIOUS ILLNESS

If you are ill, your physical preparations also involve managing the medical care you receive. The remainder of this chapter looks at your health care considerations.

❑ **Educate yourself about your illness and treatment options.**

I found that the best information in the world was available via public libraries, medical libraries, and the Internet. Not only could I find out the latest news on my disease, but the public and medical libraries had research staff who were happy to help me locate information and use the Internet for *free*. Through these resources I learned who the leading doctors were for my illness. Then, I asked my doctor for copies of my medical records, which I sent by fax or overnight mail to the two or three leading physicians I found through my research. I included a cover note to each doctor or their lead nurse, asking them if they could review my file and give me their recommendations for treatment without charging a fee for a consult. I also asked if they could forward me any articles that they thought were applicable to my case. Most doctors and nurses were very responsive and helpful.

➤ Be aggressive about getting up-to-date and accurate information. Ask lots of questions, take notes, and get all the help you can.

❑ **Find the right health care provider(s) for you.**

Since getting cancer, the only time Doug and I have felt truly angry has been with the health care system. From the beginning, Doug and I decided we would research both conventional and alternative treatment options. We quickly discovered that evaluating doctors was very difficult and frustrating. First, many doctors were not willing to answer detailed questions about their protocols and their success rates. If they did discuss success rates, many doctors were not willing to provide documentation to prove their claims. The further we probed, the more irritated these doctors became. In more than one instance, doctors became quickly defensive and unwilling to address our questions.

With very little assistance from the doctors, we started to do our own independent research on breast cancer and treatment options. We learned more about cancer and the appropriate treatment options from our own research than we did from the doctors. When we presented our findings to some doctors, they would immediately discount them and move the discussion back to their own clinical trials, protocols, and treatment recommendations. We felt we couldn't get their respect and attention, which became very frustrating.

If our research didn't aggravate the doctors enough, the fact that we wanted opinions from several doctors put some doctors over the top. One doctor told us point blank that he would not discuss his treatment options relative to any other doctor's treatment recommendations or opinions. He explained the treatment once and then absolutely refused to answer any additional questions we had for him. When we cited another doctor's concerns about his treatment strategy, he blew up. This physician got so overheated that another doctor heard our conversation through a closed door and joined our meeting to ask the original doctor to take the time to address our concerns.

Compounding the difficulty was the fact that conventional chemotherapy and radiation treatments had obvious toxicity to the body, but had statistically variable results. In other words, we knew that I would have severe and in some cases permanent side effects from the conventional treatments, and still would have only a modest chance of long-term survival. We started to research unconventional doctors and treatments, which were attractive in part because they were nontoxic. In addition, several breast cancer patients we knew decided to take unconventional treatments exclusively. They seemed to be doing fine, although they had not been taking the treatments long enough to draw any firm conclusions. With unconventional treatments, there were few, if any, published clinical trials citing the effectiveness of the protocols. All the evidence surrounding the alternative treatments was anecdotal.

The number of conventional and unconventional treatments was overwhelming. It became painfully clear there was no treatment option for my cancer that offered exceptional results. We had to be the judge and jury when it came to deciding on the best option. We were scared and unsure, especially considering we did not know the first thing about breast cancer or chemotherapy as little as thirty days prior.

At this point, Doug and I had some of the most emotional and intense discussions of our marriage. We were both distraught at the limitations and toxicity of the various treatments. We had thrown our energies into cancer research at the expense of discussing and releasing pent up emotions. We were bone-tired and our nerves were shot. Doug was anxious because our extensive research had now delayed my treatment. If the cancer was still somewhere in me, even though the only known tumor had been removed, Doug worried the delay could be life-threatening. He also felt strongly that I should go the conventional route and try the chemotherapy. At least with chemotherapy there was documented evidence that some people received substantial benefit from the drugs. Though Doug was scared of chemotherapy's side effects, he was more afraid that relying solely on unconventional treatments would be a death sentence.

The longer we waited to make the decision, the more anxious Doug became. Soon, my family and friends started to grow anxious as well. Doug began to push conventional treatment options before I felt mentally or emotionally ready. I pushed back, citing the extreme toxicity of the chemotherapy. In the end, after many tearful and sleepless nights, we decided to start a conventional treatment regime in conjunction with a number of unconventional, nontoxic treatments.

It wasn't until after the initial chemotherapy and radiation treatments that we finally found the right physician—someone with an excellent track record, a willingness to try new treatments and test for their efficacy, an interest in my questions and in collaborating with me to make treatment decisions, and a wonderful, caring way about him. It was an enormous relief. With Dr. George Blumenschein on our side, I could relax and feel infinitely more at peace with the whole health care system. At the same time, I could try alternative treatments, informing Dr. Blumenschein and seeking his counsel each step of the way.

➤ Having confidence in your health care providers is essential to your physical and emotional well-being. Don't hesitate to ask questions and get the information you need to feel certain that you are in the right hands—even if some doctors are uncomfortable with your questions. Your health is in your hands.

➤ If you cannot travel or if money is a constraint, ask respected doctors and nurses if they can recommend physicians in your area or drugs that are in clinical trial that a local doctor could administer. *Be creative* about getting the best care.

❏ **Manage your care.**

Doug and I have stopped, initiated, and modified my treatment countless times during my battle with cancer. Basically, we came to realize that I knew my body better than anybody else. Doctors might make a particular recommendation on managing the side effects of treatments but I often could better anticipate how my body would react. Doug, too, had seen me react to every treatment, every drug, and every stage of the disease. It was critical for us to be involved in deciding my treatments.

For example, after my cancer spread to my spine, I wanted to monitor the spread of the disease in my body so we could figure out how best to stymie its going forward. One doctor said he would give me blood tests only to see if the cancer had spread— when the original cancer never would have shown up on a blood test at all! Shortly thereafter, we found Dr. Blumenschein, who was willing to do more thorough scans and change my treatment regime depending on the spread of the cancer.

Now, I feel certain that one of the reasons I am alive today is because Doug, my parents, my physician and I have together so actively managed my care.

➤ Don't hold back if you think a doctor or nurse is making a wrong decision or is giving you inadequate care. Ask for what you need, and if you don't get it, look elsewhere for it.

❏ **Make decisions regarding your end-of-life medical care.**

If you are managing a terminal illness, I encourage you to ask your doctor about the difficult decisions your caregivers could expect to face if your illness progresses. Giving your caregivers your opinion on these very personal and emotionally charged issues is a gift. For your instructions to be as specific as possible, discuss with your physician what would transpire should you die from this illness. Among the questions you might ask are:

1. What would physically happen near the end of your life, ultimately causing your death?
2. What are your doctor's recommendations for end-of-life pain management and other medical treatments?
3. Would your doctor manage the process and, if not, who would?

I have heard that some physicians resist talking about how one's life might end, using the argument that "dwelling on the hard things in the future, you end up living them twice." I could not disagree more. Before I had the facts in hand, my imagination of what might happen as I died terrified me. Hearing the doctor's candid answers was a relief. No longer did this great worry disturb the quiet recesses of my mind. Also, with this information, I could anticipate the potential conflicts that could arise within my family over my end-of-life care. For example, I told Doug I wanted to try every means available to survive. That meant if my doctor found a new treatment that had the potential to extend my life—even if the treatment might cause a painful death—I would want to try it. My husband understood and agreed to adhere to my wishes.

When I told my mother the instructions I had given Doug, I knew it would be hard for her. As a mother, she felt tormented at the thought of her child in pain or distress. We had a long conversation about my end-of-life health care decisions and I wrote her a letter affirming my preferences. I wanted her to know that if I had a chance to live longer, I preferred to manage the pain and be conscious than to give up and be sedated. It was hard for her, but she appreciated having the opportunity to voice her reluctance. She also has had some time to come to terms with my plans so that, should my health deteriorate, she will not be taken by surprise with the introduction of new, potentially painful treatments.

These discussions had the important additional benefit of alleviating last minute conflicts that could have arisen between my husband and my parents over my end-of-life medical treatment. Ultimately, I hope my husband and my parents will continue to have a loving, caring friendship if I pass away.

> ➤ After discussing with your physician what would likely transpire as you near death, decide on the treatment options you prefer. I strongly suggest putting your wishes in writing to guide your appointed representative (see "Grant durable power of attorney for health care decisions," page 140). It is also advisable to notify your immediate family of your end-of-life wishes. Your family and friends might not all agree with your choices, but the decisions are yours. Your decisiveness will help preserve the peace within your family should you pass away.

❑ Research hospice facilities in your area.

If you have a terminal illness, you might be interested in receiving hospice care at the end of your life. Hospices are exceptional organizations that offer loving and quality care for people who have decided to discontinue curative treatments, and want only palliative care during their last months of life. I have known several people who were cared for by hospice workers and volunteers and were enormously pleased and grateful for the exceptional care they received.

➤ Hospice can provide care at your home or in a hospice facility, depending on your needs and preference. I recommend meeting with and interviewing the managers of the hospices in your area before you are in need of their services. The stronger you are, the better equipped you are to select the hospice that is best for you. In addition, the more you know about the hospice and the care they can and cannot give you, the easier it will be for you to project your future needs.

CHAPTER SUMMARY

❒ Decide if you will be buried or cremated.
❒ Select a cemetery.
❒ Make burial arrangements.
❒ Select your headstone and draft the inscription.
❒ Decide on an open or closed casket.
❒ Consider ways to minimize funeral costs.
❒ Make out-of-state funeral arrangements, if appropriate.
❒ Decide who will write the eulogy.
❒ Plan the service.
❒ Draft your obituary; choose a black-and-white photograph.
❒ Make additional decisions about your funeral or memorial and your burial or cremation.

If You Are Living with a Serious Illness

❏ Educate yourself about your illness and treatment options.
❏ Find the right health care provider(s) for you.
❏ Manage your care.
❏ Make decisions regarding your end-of-life medical care.
❏ Research hospice facilities in your area.

6

THE MENTAL PREPARATIONS FOR DEATH: A CONTINGENCY PLAN FOR THE FUTURE

In the last few years, I have talked with numerous people shortly after they were diagnosed with a serious illness. We all shared an almost comical initial reaction: We felt an incredible need to clean out our closets, bureaus, and file cabinets so that, in the event of our deaths, (1) others won't have to do it, (2) friends and family won't find out how really messy we were, and (3) we left our estate in order. This became an enormously distracting issue for me because there was so much to be organized, catalogued, and decided. I had a filing system no one else could decipher, and important papers that only I could locate. As I started organizing my things, I realized that my heirs could lose significant sums of money if I did not leave them accurate and up-to-date information on our bank accounts, our insurance plans and filings, our safe-deposit box contents, and our investments—not to mention plans for my estate. There were just so many loose ends.

We decided to title this chapter "The Mental Preparations for Death" because the process of organizing the details of one's life is largely a mental one. Deciding where to put things so they can be found again, creating systems for running the household, making decisions about financial and estate planning, and writing a will all demand the use of one's mental faculties. In this chapter, we have tried to make the process of organizing these details as easy and painless as possible. Please note: these mental preparations can become quite tedious if you take them on all at once. If you feel yourself getting bogged down, skip to the next chapter, and come back to this one when you feel ready.

❏ Create a household management binder.

To ease the burden on your family should you pass away, gather important household information in one place. I used a notebook binder, which I called the bluebook, to create a reference manual. With the bluebook in hand, someone could walk into my house and know how to run the household. That person would know which companies to contact for services, the doctors to call for each member of the family and the pets, and pertinent information regarding neighbors, insurance, birthdays, and other important occasions. Following is the table of contents for my bluebook:

I. EMERGENCY
    A. Emergency numbers
    B. Locations of hospitals for particular needs
    C. Authorization letter for children's medical care
    D. List of family members' doctors
    E. Wills and durable power of attorney

II. LOCATION OF MASTER LIST OF DOCUMENTS
    A. Filing cabinets
    B. Office
    C. Safe
    D. Warranties and instructions
    E. Calendar of family birthdays

III. HOUSEHOLD MANAGEMENT AND AGREEMENTS
    A. Heating, A/C, electrical, and plumbing
    B. Lawn care and pool maintenance

C. Pet records and care
D. Car dealership (for car maintenance)
E. Watering plants
F. How to prepare the house for guests
G. Going out-of-town instructions

IV. FOOD MANAGEMENT

A. Staples for house from grocery store
B. Sample weekly menus and recipes
C. Staples from wholesale club
D. Staples for pets

V. CHILDREN'S SCHEDULES

A. Weekly schedule and location of activities
B. Daily schedule
C. Playmates
D. Authorized baby sitters and procedure
E. Location of caregiver's contract and questionnaire

VI. DIRECTORY OF FAMILY AND FRIENDS

This directory can be used for the holiday mailing list, or in the event of the death of a family member, to notify friends and family of the date and time of service.

❏ **Organize the documents that will be needed at the end of life.**

Each document listed below is needed near the end of life. To organize and store the reams of paper, I bought a large accordian file with alphabetized dividers. That way, should my health deteriorate or I pass away, Doug will know the logistics are organized and under control. He will not have to search for important documents when he has much more pressing things on his mind.

➤ In addition to the documents listed later in this chapter, develop and/or gather these documents:

- Your birth certificate (approximately five copies are needed)
- Your social security card
- Your marriage license
- Your citizenship papers, if appropriate
- Preplanned funeral arrangements
- Burial property certificate of ownership
- Documents authorizing anatomical gifts
- Your insurance policies (life, health, disability, burial, and property)
- Disability claims, if any
- Death benefits from employer
- Military discharge papers, if appropriate
- Income tax returns for the prior two years
- Your back account numbers, passbooks, and addresses
- List of all credit cards, including gas, with account numbers and passwords
- Location of safety-deposit boxes and keys
- Details on all investments, including brokerage accounts, stocks, and real estate
- Any deed(s) to property you own
- Your automobile bill of sale and/or title
- Details on all debts

❏ **Write down your vital statistics for reference.**
- Your name, home address, and telephone number
- How long you have lived at the current address
- Your workplace address and telephone number
- Your occupation
- Your social security number
- Your armed services number, if appropriate
- Your date and place of birth
- Your father's name and birthplace
- Your mother's maiden name and birthplace
- Names and addresses of your heirs

- Names and numbers of your personal physicians
- Names and numbers of professional advisors

❑ **Write your will.**

Doug and I worked with an attorney to write our wills so we could be certain our wishes were properly articulated and we abided by state laws. Also, we knew that once we engaged an attorney to work on our wills with us, the project would get finished. Left to our own devices, we might have been distracted by other, more immediate projects.

➤ If, like us, you wish to use an attorney to draft your will, ask the attorney up front about the fees and expenses associated with his or her services. Agree with your attorney on the fee before asking for legal advice. If you prefer to write your will without professional assistance, your local library or bookstore probably carries kits with templates and instructions for creating a valid will. With these prepackaged wills we still recommend consulting with an attorney to finalize the document because sometimes these store-bought versions do not comply with state laws.

❑ **Select the executor of your will.**

Before we selected the executor of our wills, we did not realize the enormous responsibilities involved. The executor is the person responsible for managing our estate if someone passes away. Among the responsibilities are:

- Making sure the stipulations of the will were carried out
- Submitting the tax forms for the estate
- Notifying government agencies, vendors, and others of the death
- Paying bills (particularly complicated if health-care reimbursements are involved)
- A myriad of other details

Learning about the executor's duties greatly influenced our selection process. Ultimately, we asked two dear friends to serve as executor. They happen to be attorneys and are knowledgeable about the duties involved. Choosing a lawyer as executor is not necessary, but choosing someone who is responsible and competent is.

> ➤ Selecting the executor of your will is an important decision. Choose someone you trust completely and who has the capacity to manage the responsibilities of the position. I recommend asking your attorney for a list of the executor's responsibilities that you can review with the person you designate. Talk about these responsibilities with the person you designate before finalizing your will. If you like, share with them a copy of your will so they might ask any questions they might have.

❏ **Write your living will.**

Both Doug and I created living wills, which detail our wishes for future medical care in the event that either one of us cannot speak for ourselves. We worked with our attorney to spell out our wishes exactly, and for me, as my condition has changed, we have occasionally updated my living will to include more specific directives.

As I have stated elsewhere, the decisions made immediately before one's death can be the hardest for loved ones. These decisions, if not carefully outlined ahead of time, can cause a great deal of tension between family members. A detailed living will, which includes your desires on pain management and food allocation, can greatly reduce conflicts.

> ➤ In writing your living will, I suggest the following steps:

> 1. Talk with your attorney, your physician, your family members, and/or close friend about your wishes. Ask your attorney to inform you of relevant state laws.

2. Put your wishes in writing, being as specific as possible. Sign and date your living will (and witnessed and notarized, if required in your state).
3. Keep a card in your wallet stating that you have signed a living will and where it can be found.
4. Give a copy to your attorney, your physician, and someone who is likely to be notified in an emergency.
5. Keep a copy of your living will in a safe spot that is easily accessible by you and whoever you choose to share it with.
6. Review your living will regularly; update it if necessary.

❏ **Develop an estate plan.**

Though my husband's and my estate is not sizable, we have taken steps to minimize estate costs and taxes in the event of my death. Without an estate plan—essentially a plan for the transfer of a person's property should that person die—your family, friends, and favorite charities could receive significantly less than you intend for them. We decided to work with a financial planner for several reasons: (1) the laws regarding estate taxes change regularly, and I do not have the expertise or the energy to keep up with the revisions; (2) since becoming ill, I have found concentrating on these details to be difficult; and (3) I realized I was more likely actually to complete an estate plan if I had the help of a professional. With our advisor, we have devised a plan that minimizes estate settlement costs, death taxes, and the expenses associated with probate should I pass away.

As a side note, a friend who is an estate planner recently lost his business partner. His partner actually died of a heart attack while sitting at his desk working on his own estate plan. Because he passed away without finishing his work, the changes he made to his estate plan were considered incomplete and invalid. The family had to get a special dispensation to implement his wishes as he had articulated them that fateful night. Again, we never know when our time will come.

➤ There are any number of reasons to review your estate plan regularly: tax laws change; estates grow and shrink; minors become adults; people marry, divorce, move out of state, and have children. If you have a large estate, review it every year. If your estate is small, every five years should suffice.

❑ **Create your financial plan.**

I have always known that financial planning is important, but have done very little about it. It has only been with my illness that both Doug and I have realized how very important it is. Good planning can mean the difference between a comfortable lifestyle and having to scrimp to get by. And that's if everyone is healthy. Throw in a serious illness, and finances can become a terrible burden. When my cancer spread to my spine three years ago, I stopped working. At the time, I was earning an excellent income that was an important component of our family finances. Then, with only one salary, Doug and I had to plan carefully to manage all the expenses associated with my care and our household. It has been a stretch, but we have managed, partially because we received good advice and put a financial plan in place early on.

For me, completing the estate and financial planning was time-consuming and not particularly interesting. I was a finance major in college so numbers, planning, and forecasting came relatively easily to me, but with the onslaught of chemotherapy drugs, my ability to process simple equations dwindled. I forced myself to get through this because I knew there was always the chance that Doug could pass away before I did, leaving Peyton and me in financial ruin if these issues weren't addressed.

➤ Any form of prolonged illness, no matter how much insurance you have, will have a negative impact on your financial well-being and estate. We recommend talking to a financial advisor who can help you evaluate your short-

and long-term financial options. Do this as soon as you can. Your financial security over time could hinge on making sound decisions now.

❏ Obtain life insurance.

Deciding whether to buy life insurance and what type of policy to purchase can be a complicated decision—and the insurance companies seem to enjoy making things as complicated as possible! When Doug and I were both healthy, we arranged to purchase life insurance policies based on our calculations of the amount of money the remaining spouse would require to live comfortably if one of us were to die. At a minimum, we wanted the life insurance policies to cover the lost salaries, the remaining mortgage payments on the house, Peyton's education and child care costs, in addition to any other outstanding debts. By adding up our estimates for each of these expense items, we came up with the amount of insurance we needed.

As it turned out, our insurance agent delayed the processing of our policy for a month, in the hope that he could get better rates for us. During that month, we discovered I had cancer, and became ineligible for the life insurance policy we had selected. What a terrible surprise this was! The lesson we learned is not to allow any delays if having life insurance would be critical to the well-being of the policy holder's survivors.

Insurance companies offer policies with elaborate investment vehicles and which make projections for enormous amounts of wealth that the policies will generate over time. We decided to avoid these expensive policies for several reasons: the fee structures for investing were very expensive; we thought we could get better returns investing our own money; and over time, we planned to reduce the amount of life insurance we purchased. Once our mortgage was paid off and Peyton's education paid for, we would need significantly less insurance. By that time, we hoped to have saved enough money so the remaining family members could live comfortably if either of us died. For Doug, we went with what is called renewable term life insurance, the least expensive type of life insurance that gave us the flexibility to change our policy as our needs for insurance changed.

➤ Research and invest in a life insurance policy that meets the needs of your loved ones should you die. Calculate what those needs might be so that you buy neither too much nor too little life insurance.

❏ **Grant durable power of attorney to someone you trust completely.**

Granting someone power of attorney is an important step. Should you become too ill to manage your affairs, your family may be unable to deposit income checks, liquidate assets to pay bills, or pay for hospital or nursing home care on your behalf. If you have not granted power of attorney to someone and are unable to communicate your wishes, your family may be forced to apply to the court for appointment of a guardian or conservator. These court proceedings are expensive, and frequently, the guardian/conservator will have to make annual accountings to the court.

➤ Review with your lawyer the different types of power of attorney. If you are comfortable with the power of attorney options, pre-printed power of attorney forms are available in most states and can be executed without legal advice. Since the power of attorney grants significant authority, choose someone you trust completely for the position.

❏ **Grant durable power of attorney for health care decisions.**

Granting someone durable power of attorney for health care decisions and detailing your desires on pain management and food allocation can greatly reduce family conflicts. (Please note that durable power of attorney for health care decisions is different from financial power of attorney.)

It is important to be as specific as possible when it comes to detailing your end-of-life health care wishes. When Doug's mother was struggling through the last weeks of her life, Doug, his father, and brother faced difficult decisions regarding how aggressive they wanted the doctors to be in terms of prolonging her life. Having to make decisions about feeding tubes, respirators, pain medicine, and surgeries was difficult because they had to guess what treatment Doug's mother would have wanted. In the end, they wished they had discussed these issues in detail with her when she could have articulated her preferences.

IF YOU ARE LIVING WITH A SERIOUS ILLNESS

❏ Consider setting up a living trust.

If you have reason to believe you might be disabled for some time, consider setting up a living trust, which allows a trustee to step in and manage the trust property. These trusts are considerably more expensive than a durable power of attorney, so consult your attorney to review the costs and benefits.

❏ Get the support you need to handle health insurance claims.

Managing the continuous flow of paperwork associated with being ill can be overwhelming. Insurance carriers, physician's offices, hospitals, clinics, and pharmacies all have their own forms that can be confusing, especially since often they are received months following the date the service was actually provided. Doug and I have come across several reputable organizations and individuals that handle the insurance filings for patients, charging a fee for their service. If you have a long-term illness requiring extensive medical care, it might be worthwhile to engage someone to help with your insurance claims. Oftentimes, you can save money because these service providers can be skilled at ensuring their clients get the most coverage from their insurance companies. If you prefer, you might ask a friend who is organized, knowledgeable, and reliable to assist you with your claims.

IF YOU ARE A PARENT OR GRANDPARENT

❏ **Apply for Social Security disability benefits for you and your children.**

As I mention later, Doug and I feel strongly that hiring a caregiver for your children is important if a parent might pass away. However, the cost of hiring someone could be prohibitive for many people. I suggest, if you have not already done so, applying for Social Security disability benefits for yourself and your children. Children are eligible for Social Security Benefits until they reach their nineteenth birthdays or attend college, whichever comes first. In addition, Social Security offers a quick claim process for the terminally ill. These extra funds might make child care more affordable.

❏ **Decide who will take care of your children if you are a single parent or if both you and your spouse were to pass away.**

Six months after a friend of mine learned she had cancer, her husband was also diagnosed with the disease. He died six months later, and she was left to plan for the care of her children if she were to pass away. A family from her church volunteered to take care of her children permanently in the event of her death. Unfortunately, after she died, the arrangement with this family did not work out well. The children were unhappy, and one of her best friends had to step in to take over the children's upbringing. She is now in the process of adopting them.

➤ Solicit the aid of a counselor from an adoption agency to walk you through the process of finding a person or family that is the best match for your philosophy on bringing up your children.

❏ **When selecting a caregiver for your child, ask questions to ascertain the morals and values the caregiver will impart to your child.**

In chapter 4 I explained why Doug and I decided to hire a full-time caregiver for Peyton now, while I am alive. Before selecting Peyton's caregiver, I put together a lengthy questionnaire for the candidates to fill out (see Appendix A) because I wanted to know as much as possible about their approaches to child development, their morals and values, and their backgrounds. What traits did they think were important to instill in a child? What were their thoughts on discipline? In the questionnaire, I asked them to write out their answers so I could learn how they thought and how they articulated their viewpoints. For the final candidates, Doug and I had lengthy conversations with each of their references, talking about their personalities, reliability, and work ethic. We asked for specific examples of things each candidate had done exceptionally well and things he or she could have done better. We asked how they handled constructive criticism and if they were good listeners. My rule of thumb was: "History repeats itself." More specifically, an individual's history or past resume was generally a good indicator of future behavior. In the end, we wanted to find someone who was emotionally stable and could also handle getting to know me as a terminally ill patient who might die.

➤ I recommend thoroughly screening your caregiver before inviting him or her into your household. The caregiver will become an important person in your lives. You will want someone who is likable, trustworthy, pleasant, hardworking, dependable, and caring, and who is generous with his or her emotions.

❏ **Discuss with the caregiver how you would like your death and your thoughts on life after death explained to your children, in the event of your passing.**

As I mentioned earlier, it is important to let your caregiver know your thoughts on death and dying. Once we selected a caregiver, we talked with her about our belief in heaven and the conversations about life and death we had had with Peyton. We made certain not to rush this conversation. Instead, we spent an evening talking together about our views on my possible death and how Doug and I hoped to raise Peyton as normally as possible, given my ongoing health issues. Our conversation ranged to include such topics as what we would say to Peyton if I faced a health care emergency, how we organized our schedules so my treatments interrupted her routine as little as possible, and the role we hoped our caregiver would play in our daughter's and our lives. We specifically asked if she felt comfortable with our approach to death and dying and if she would feel comfortable imparting similar views to Peyton. Our lengthy conversation and her answers to our questions gave us confidence that she would be a suitable and loving caregiver for Peyton.

❏ **Select someone to care for your children immediately following your death.**

Select an emotionally stable person who is liked and well known by your children to be responsible for them during the entire funeral process—from the time of death through possible gatherings after the service. Designating the caregiver for your children is important because typically the remaining parent is flooded with decisions, responsibilities, and the attention of well-wishers. The caregiver should be totally available to supervise the children and accommodate their needs. It is important for the caregiver to know that the children may want to eat, play or ask questions—all of which are appropriate. Children react differently to tragedy. Some of the ways a child might react are:

- Expressing anger, sadness, shock, or surprise
- Appearing not to feel anything
- Withdrawing
- Expressing feelings of guilt

Often children will react by turning their attention else-where—to games or food or other distractions—and this is a normal part of the grieving process for them. It is important for adults never to say to children that they didn't look sad. Judgments of this kind by adults hurt children.

CHAPTER SUMMARY

- ❏ Create a household management binder.
- ❏ Organize the documents that will be needed at the end of life.
- ❏ Write down your vital statistics for reference.
- ❏ Write your will.
- ❏ Select the executor of your will.
- ❏ Write your living will.
- ❏ Develop an estate plan.
- ❏ Create your financial plan.
- ❏ Obtain life insurance.
- ❏ Grant durable power of attorney to someone you trust completely.
- ❏ Grant durable power of attorney for health care decisions.

If You Are Living with a Serious Illness
- ❏ Consider setting up a living trust.
- ❏ Get the support you need to handle health insurance claims.

If You Are a Parent or Grandparent
- ❏ Apply for Social Security disability benefits for you and your children.

❑ Decide who will take care of your children if you are a single parent or if both you and your spouse were to pass away.

❑ When selecting a caregiver for your child, ask questions to ascertain the morals and values the caregiver will impart to your child.

❑ Discuss with the caregiver how you would like your death and your thoughts on life after death explained to your children, in the event of your passing.

❑ Select someone to care for your children immediately following your death.

7

PREPARE SPIRITUALLY: FINDING YOUR OWN PATH

Our deepest fear is not that we are inadequate. Our deepest fear is that we are powerful beyond measure. It is our light, not our darkness, that most frightens us. We ask ourselves, who am I to be so brilliant, gorgeous, talented, and fabulous? Actually, who are we not to be? You are a child of God. Your playing small doesn't serve the world. There is nothing enlightened about shrinking so that other people won't feel insecure around you. We were born to make manifest the glory of God that is within us. It's not just in some of us; it's in everyone. And as we let our own light shine, we unconsciously give other people permission to do the same. As we are liberated from our own fear, our presence automatically liberates others.

MARIANNE WILLIAMSON,
A Return to Love

I have often heard the question, "How do you differentiate between the spirit and the mind?" I think of my mind—which reflects a lifetime of learning, the ability to process information, and even some creativity as being stored in my brain. Once the blood supply is removed, my brain will stop functioning and deteriorate. In contrast, my spirit is the essence of my being, a composite of energy and love, that continues to resonate with the life-giving force of a higher being. For me, that higher being is God.

When I was young, I felt a strong connection to my spiritual side. As I grew up, however, my mind and emotions began to dominate my thinking, and I let my spirituality recede. By the time I became an adult, I was accustomed to using my mental processes—problem solving, analyzing, thinking things through—to handle whatever came my way. This approach worked well for me, but only up to a point. I had a great career, a husband I loved, and a delightful daughter, yet I felt there was something missing. I had the nagging feeling that there had to be something more to my life. For years, I asked myself what God's purpose was for me. I wanted to devote my energies and passions to something I believed in and that gave me fulfillment. I admired Mother Teresa, who lived her life according to clearly stated beliefs and commitments. For myself, however, I saw any number of different paths I could take. Should I give up my career in venture capital to join a worthwhile cause? Should I give all my money to charity? Should I run a nonprofit? Choosing the right path became a seemingly insurmountable problem.

At the time, I thought I could reason my way to an answer, that my life's purpose would come to me through a rational, intellectual inquiry. It did not occur to me that my spiritual side could illuminate my purpose in life, or that I could integrate spirituality into my everyday life. Doug encouraged me to be more flexible in trying to blend my spiritual side with my business life, but I couldn't merge the two. I saw things as all or nothing. The thought of allowing my spiritual side to have a say in my life choices was a hugely unfamiliar and frightening prospect. If I had done so, my illusion of control would have been shattered. At least by using my mental processes to define a calling for myself, I could control the outcome. I could expect to reason my way to answers and hold the reins when making important decisions about my life.

As it turned out, the answer was right around the corner for me. As I have mentioned earlier in the book, not long after the cancer spread to my spine, I contracted an infection in my intestine and abdomen, which almost took my life. For three weeks, I was secluded in a bubble room, barely conscious while my husband and parents stayed by my side day and night, all the while thinking I was about to die.

While my body was fighting for its life, my spirit was in another place. In the tranquillity of that room, I began a spiritual journey. In that meditative state, my mind stopped chattering, and I heard what God had to say to me. I remember saying I felt unworthy of His attention. Who was I to have a conversation with God? With His answers, I came to see that my feelings of inadequacy came from me, not Him. He was standing there with open arms at all times. I could choose to be more like Him or I could choose otherwise. Each and every day, I had this enormous freedom to choose. God taught me that each of us has a unique prism through which His love is reflected to those around us. It did not matter *what* I did in my life, whether I swept floors, became a surgeon, created companies, or gave all my money to charity. What mattered was not what I did, but *how I did it*. Did I allow God's love to flow through me as I lived every day? Was I compassionate, and did I touch the souls of the people around me? My purpose, as simple as it seemed, was to allow God's love to flow through me.

My sense of purpose did not stem from a rational analysis of the options available to me. I did not evaluate my life based on my present circumstances with an eye to the future, which had been my old way of problem solving. Instead, I envisioned my life coming to an end, reviewing my life with God, and then worked backward. In this shift, intellectualizing did not work. My spirit led the way. I did not need to make things more complicated than they were because ironically, the most beautiful things in life are simple.

When I pulled through the infection on Easter morning, I remember my doctor putting his head on my chest and saying,

"Thank you, Lord." I was going to live, and for us, it was a miracle in answer to all the prayers of our friends and family on that Easter day. I had been through this incredible spiritual experience, and it looked as if I was going to be around for a while. At first, it was hard to think of leaving the bubble room. In the sanctity of that room, I had come so close to God and had felt His love so deeply. I wondered what I would do next. Would I be able to maintain this spiritual connection? How would I act on what I had learned? And how could I possibly implement my purpose while I was confined to a hospital room? At last, I knew what my life was about, but I was afraid I wouldn't have a chance to live my life according to what I had discovered.

As I thought about this, I realized I could reach out to people, one soul at a time. If all I did was to improve someone's day or lighten a person's load, I would be living according to my purpose. Perhaps I could reach out to people, one person at a time. Since then, I have seen and felt the impact we all have on each other. As I let God's love flow through me, my priorities became clear.

As it turned out, my disease was a catalyst for both Doug and me to get closer to God, though we followed different spiritual paths. Knowing I might die from cancer, I turned to God for sustenance, peace, and healing. Doug, however, needed strength and peace of mind to handle the burdens placed on him, which were unrelenting. Doug had to answer some tough questions for himself, among them:

- What would he do if I were to die?
- How would he raise our daughter without me?
- How could he balance our daughter's and my needs as well as his career?
- What is the purpose of his life?
- What was the purpose of suffering?
- Where would he find strength and hope when he was so utterly tired?
- What did God want him to learn from this experience?

Before my cancer, Doug had an "on-call" relationship with God. In other words, when his life was going smoothly and his schedule got too full, he wouldn't take the time to "call." When he ran into challenges or hardships, he would "call in" God until his life got back on track. This system worked until I got sick. Then, Doug's usual mode of operating—relying primarily on himself and occasionally turning to God—didn't work for him. He got completely worn out—emotionally, physically, and spiritually. When it reached a point that he wasn't sure he could handle it all, Doug turned to God for strength and for answers.

Doug started praying often and intensively. For the first time, Doug offered up his questions, fears, and exhaustion to God. By literally turning everything over to Him, Doug felt an immediate sense of relief. It took some time for his relationship with God to develop, but as time progressed, his prayers started to be answered. His concerns about me, Peyton, and the rest of his life became more manageable. Doug's big breakthrough came when he realized the challenges he faced were his path to character and spiritual development. The tough times were not meaningless ends in themselves, but rather, a means of getting closer to God. He had a choice. He could let the hardships beat him down, or he could embrace them. Doug saw for the first time that he had been given a unique opportunity to grow both spiritually and emotionally. As he took on more and endured more, Doug could turn to God for His support and, in so doing, build a relationship with God that was intimate, honest and reliable.

Looking back on the last four years, Doug says there was no way he could have handled it all without his relationship with God. Despite everything he has been through, his life has flourished. He and I are closer than ever; he's received several promotions; our daughter is balanced and happy; and Doug is in better physical shape than he's ever been. Both of us are convinced we could not have weathered the last few years so well without God's hand holding us up.

Only through our spiritual selves did Doug and I achieve a sense of inner peace and well-being. As we integrated the spiritual with the physical, mental, and emotional, we achieved a balance and happiness we had never felt before. Thereafter, when our spiritual dimensions were off balance or neglected, our whole beings suffered. We have come to believe that our internal joy at the time of death rests primarily on our spiritual well-being. To paraphrase the writer Teilhard de Chardin, "We think we are human beings having a spiritual experience, when in truth, we are spiritual beings having a human experience." It was not until we faced death that we allowed our spiritual sides to reflect our souls' purposes.

➤ Preparing oneself spiritually does not necessarily mean choosing a religion. Ultimately, focusing on your spiritual side means taking time to define your beliefs, meditate and pray, and reflect on your purpose in the world. The exceptional opportunity of spiritual reflection, available to us all, is to live our lives with a sense of purpose.

➤ I invite you to use this chapter to explore your spiritual underpinnings and to dive in and enjoy the process of discovery. No one is looking over your shoulder or trying to impose a particular religious dogma on you. Here you have a chance to decide—to really choose—your spiritual tenets in the context of the inevitability of your death. Think of this chapter as an opportunity to discover the greatest gift of all, inner peace.

➤ If you are terminally ill and are reading this book, you will find it easier to visualize the end of your life and work through the Spiritual Checklist than if you are healthy. For the healthy, you will need to imagine your life coming to an end. Really. Take time to think about your spiritual beliefs in the context of eternity, knowing that when you die your spiritual beliefs may have real implications.

❏ Decide if you believe in a higher being.

If you are unsure whether you believe in a higher being or have decided hastily, I recommend doing some homework. Your belief in, or denial of, a higher being is an essential component of your spiritual character. From this question all further spiritual exploration follows. In your search, here are some things you might want to consider:

1. Read books and papers and medical articles on life after death. Doctors have collected data and interviewed hundreds of people who have died medically and then regained their lives. Their impressions of the transition from life to death are remarkably consistent and all reflect a belief in life after death.

2. Ask a local hospice if you can volunteer with a dying patient. The reason I suggest this is that among all the people I know who work in hospices, I have never met an agnostic. These dedicated caregivers did not necessarily believe in God when they started working in hospice, but their patients convinced them there is a God. By being with people as they have died, the caregivers felt the presence of the spirit leaving the physical body at the time of death. You cannot feel that from a book, but you can feel that from the dying.

3. Look inward. Take time to reflect, to try to feel God's presence in your life.

❏ Decide whether you believe in a separation of body and spirit.

Another way to pose this question is: Do you believe there is a soul that will live on beyond the life of your body? Some people believe they have a spirit that lives on after they physically die. These people can actually feel and sense their spirit. Others do not believe in a spirit at all. If you do not fall into either of these categories or are unsure, then challenge yourself to define your beliefs. As with the previous checklist item, take time to decide what you believe regarding this question. If you don't know the answer for yourself, the remainder of the checklist might assist you in making a decision.

❏ Establish your own personal relationship with God.

Just as scientists have proven that plants grow more during storms than in sunshine, a friend once said it was easier to have a strong relationship with God when there was a crisis. It was during good times, when things were going well, that it was difficult to maintain a close connection to God. How true.

Most of my life, I have prayed only sporadically, without much thought or consistency. My prayers generally centered on saying The Lord's Prayer, expressing gratitude for the day's activities and love, asking forgiveness of sins, and asking Him to watch over loved ones in need. I certainly did not allocate the time and energy that could have led to a deep relationship with God.

After first getting cancer and facing the possibility I could die from the disease, I made it a priority to establish a relationship with God. I wanted to feel spiritually at peace with the prospect of my death, and I saw my connection to God as the avenue to that peace. But first, I had to get over my fears and uncertainties about God. I had many of them.

1. Would I ever learn to quiet my mind's chatter and look inside myself for answers?
2. If I let my spirituality take precedence, would my life change in unpredictable ways?
3. What would my colleagues, friends, and family think?
4. Would I have to answer to a higher being, rather than just to me?

My apprehensions and doubts weighed heavily. Ultimately, I decided the best approach was to ask God for answers; I didn't have to go it alone in this search. I started praying for answers. As I listened to God, I began to receive answers to my questions and fully understand that what was important was my relationship with Him.

➤ If you do not already have a relationship with God, the idea of establishing one might feel strange or unprecedented. I encourage you to give it a try, particularly if you are feeling disconnected from God, alone, or spiritually empty. A relationship with God can have only positive effects.

➤ Remember, this is your private conversation with yourself. If this is unfamiliar terrain, give yourself leeway to feel uncomfortable. Take time to reflect and try to feel God's presence. Over time, see if your thoughts and feelings about God shift in any way.

➤ Doug's analogy for a relationship with God is plugging into a wall socket. If you imagine God's energy to be like electricity that flows through the world, then you have only to plug into it to get the charge. It's there, available to each one of us, but it is up to us to make the first move.

❑ **Write down any questions or fears you have about God.**

Prior to the bubble room, I had conceptual disagreements about God. For example, I had never reconciled my early religious teachings with my own thoughts on spirituality. Religious dogma was often at odds with my view of the world. The concept that was particularly problematic was the idea, espoused by numerous religions, that there is only one way to God—their way. If you didn't believe in and follow the teachings of each of these religions, you would be doomed never to reach God. The exclusivity of this stance kept me from exploring my own beliefs. How could different religions possibly state unequivocally that they knew who would join God in heaven? I decided to pray on this question. In turn, I received a strong message from God not to be distracted by the religious viewpoints of others, but to concentrate on exploring and defining my own beliefs. I was to find my own path and work on establishing my own deep relationship with Him. Others would find their way to God, following their individual spiritual pathways.

To communicate effectively with God, first, I wrote down the issues I could think of, which identified the areas of uncertainty that were standing between me and God. I organized the list according to questions that interested me and ones that created real stumbling blocks. To address these issues, I did some soul searching, took time to meditate and pray on the questions, read my religion's holy writings, and sought the counsel of spiritual advisors. Ultimately, listening to God with an open heart provided me the clearest answers.

> ➤ This process can be particularly difficult if your relationship with God takes you down a different spiritual path than that of your loved ones and/or family. Remember this is ultimately your soul's pathway and is not a group decision.

❏ Learn and take time to meditate.

In order to have a "conversation with God," I needed to quiet my mind. When I sat back to listen to God, all I heard was what I didn't what to hear: incessant chatter about "stuff," busywork, things to get done, minor aspects of human relationships, self-doubts, feelings of unworthiness in God's eyes, and fears of the unknown. Learning to shut down this internal dialogue took time. I had to work up to it slowly and not become frustrated. When I meditated, I concentrated on not thinking, on reaching a state of mental nothingness and clarity. First, I listened outside myself to the noises around me. Then, I focused on my own breathing. With my eyes closed, I tried to create a blank slate in my mind. I did this for short periods of time, say a minute or two, throughout the course of the day until I worked up to longer periods of time.

❏ Pray.

What is the difference between meditation and prayer? I see prayer as a conversation with God, while meditation can involve simply quiet contemplation. For me, prayer involves praise for God and thanks for blessings received, although not everyone would agree. The real point of prayer is to talk to God. He wants you to talk to Him in any form.

To pray, I first sought to achieve a quiet state of mind so that I could listen and/or pray, much like meditation. My next challenge was to distinguish between my own voice and messages from God. This was not easy since my mind likes to control things. However, when I listened fully to my heart and soul, I heard a voice of knowledge and love, or had sudden inner wisdom that I knew did not come from me. The message would simply ring true, would not be self-serving, and would invariably bring me closer to God. The ultimate challenge was not hearing or feeling the message, but taking action on what was spoken.

My time for prayer has been at night. I take a hot bath, settle into bed, and pray to God that He present me with the things I need to learn. Then I hold my Bible, repeat the prayer, and randomly open the Bible. I read what is written on the page opened, and invariably, the lesson is completely clear. Finally, I mark my place and write in my journal what I've discovered.

Some people like to pray in the morning, though I have found it to be more difficult to clear my mind then. I start each day with more simple prayers, such as thanking God for another day. At midday, following or preceding lunch, I try to take a five-minute break for quiet and prayer.

> ➤ I understand that even the greatest spiritual leaders sometimes have difficulty getting in sync with prayer. At times, prayer flows easily and naturally and at other times you might feel stagnant and stuck. The trick is to keep trying.

❑ **If you are married, say nightly prayers aloud with your spouse.**

Praying together has been one of the most intimate experiences I have shared with my husband. This idea was recommended to us by a dear friend who has prayed aloud with his wife for over twenty years. At first, when we tried it, Doug and I felt uncomfortable and unnatural praying aloud. We kept at it, though, and it wasn't long before our prayers together became a great source of strength. Both Doug and I saw our horizons expand and our understanding of each other come into greater focus by praying together. Over time, our prayers shifted in noticeable ways as we came to terms with our mortality and established closer relationships with God. There have even been times when one of us has felt disconnected from God and has found strength in the other's prayers. Also, sometimes one of us feels too tired to pray. In that case, the other person prays, sparking the prayerful connection to God in us both.

> ➤ If you want to strengthen your marriage or work through difficult times, praying aloud together and soliciting God's help can be tremendously healing.

❏ Pray with your children.

Traditionally, we say prayers with our daughter before each meal and before her bedtime. When we pray together at night, each of us talks aloud to God, thanking Him for His many blessings and asking Him to look after our loved ones and give us strength and peace in our lives. When we first started saying prayers together, Peyton would tend to copy what we said in our prayers. She wasn't sure how to pray and she didn't feel comfortable doing it on her own. Over time, though, she gradually started saying her own prayers, and now they cover her innermost spiritual reflections. Sometimes we light a prayer candle, lower the lights, and sit around the candle praying together. At other times, when I am not feeling well, just Doug and Peyton say evening prayers around the prayer candle. Lighting the prayer candle became a tradition in our house after a friend gave us the idea and our first candle.

We have found that listening to our daughter's prayers brings us closer to God. Her conversations are so pure and loving that she opens our hearts to feel more of God's goodness in our lives. After praying together, we all have felt a serenity in our household that is unavailable in any other way.

❏ **Be patient with your spiritual development.**

I have had to be patient in my relationship with God. Sometimes, it has been easy to feel a connection to Him and to reach a point of inner peace and tranquillity. At other times, for the life of me, I have been unable to relax and hear what He had to say to me or feel his presence in my life. This seems natural. Doug says that working through the times when communication is difficult can give a relationship with God additional depth and meaning. Some of the most spiritual people I know tell me they are not "on" every time they seek to pray. So it is with me.

➤ Several people have expressed their impatience with God, wanting a close relationship to appear instantly. We talked about this phenomenon and realized something funny. For some reason, we tend to treat a relationship with God differently than we would one with a person we meet for the first time. With a person, we give it time, allowing a relationship to develop slowly until a deep-seated trust had been established. With God, we try to rush a relationship, when with others, we allow more leeway. Once we start looking at God as someone with whom their relationship could deepen over time, we can relax and let ourselves feel comfortable with the relationship. Over time, the closeness and connection can come.

❏ **Look for God's work in your life.**

Doug and I have gained strength by looking for and finding signs of God's love in our lives. Once we starting looking, we found His presence everywhere.

Late one night I started to shake uncontrollably. We weren't sure of the cause, whether is was the cancer, the chemotherapy or some related fever, and we were frightened. Doug tried everything to calm me down, from massaging me to lying on top of me trying to hold my limbs down. When nothing seemed to work, Doug asked God to calm my body. Immediately, my shaking stopped.

> ➤ Look for signs of God's goodness and healing touch. I don't mean set up tests for Him (such as, if you do this, I'll believe in you). A relationship with God (or with anyone, for that matter) cannot be based on that kind of test. Look at your world differently, in the hopes of catching glimpses of His helping hand. Give yourself a chance to see something you have not seen before.

❑ Read your religion's holy works.

Until a few years ago, Doug and I had never gone to the source of Christian teachings and examined the writings on our own. Ironically, in my interest in studying the world's religions, I had read the holy works from many other religions before I read the Bible, which was central to my faith. With the birth of our daughter, Doug and I decided to learn more about our spiritual roots. We signed up for a course in which we read the Bible, cover to cover. Throughout the course, discussion stimulated many ideas. We had an engaging teacher and an interesting group of students who shared our interest in finding answers to our many questions. The conversations in class cleared up many of my cloudy areas about religious doctrine. Reading the Bible and taking the course were a watershed for me. I found the New Testament to be a tremendous resource and inspiration.

❑ Learn about the religions of the world.

I have learned a great deal by reading the works of other religions. By exploring the core beliefs of different religions, I found there were key themes, messages from God and commandments in all three of the world's major religions: Islam, Christianity, and Judaism. When I worked with The Dallas Kindness Foundation, we studied the fourteen religions practiced in Dallas, including several smaller religions. Based on our analysis and with the approval of the local religions' leaders, we summarized the common tenets of the religions.[5]

- Do unto others as you would have them do unto you.
- Give that you may receive.
- Honor your mother and father.
- Love so that you may be loved.
- Share your heart so that others may know love.
- Through prayer and meditation, spiritual enlightenment is obtained.
- One is known by one's deeds, not by one's religion.
- Showing compassion creates a conduit for love.
- Prayer is the most powerful tool we possess.
- Forgive so that you may be forgiven.
- Be slow to anger.
- Conquer with love, not violence.
- Fasting is good for the body and soul.
- Give and love unconditionally.
- Judge not, lest you be judged.
- Blessed are the peacemakers.
- Do not steal.
- Smile.
- Be kind.
- Do not lie.
- Do not kill.
- Praise.

These commonalities provide a hope for religious tolerance in the world.

❏ Find a spiritual advisor or mentor.

I have routinely asked myself spiritual questions for which I have been unable to find answers. In these instances, I have turned to several "spiritual advisors"—trained and knowledge-

---

5. 1997 Faith Committee of The Dallas Kindness Foundation.

able leaders who agreed to guide my spiritual growth. Among them is Don Benton, whose insights and responses to our questions have opened new doors and helped us delve deeper into our spirituality. In some ways, these advisors have been my coaches. (And, I have come to learn, even my coaches have coaches!)

❏ **Allocate time to spend with people who exude spiritual strength.**

Since becoming ill, I have been surprised by the spiritual strength of my friends and family. Prior to my illness, I had no idea how deeply spiritual the people around me were. All of us had been so painfully private about our spiritual struggles and growth and learning processes. We tended not to share our thoughts even with the people closest to us. What a loss of fellowship for us all! My illness has spurred my family, friends and me to be more open about our individual spiritual walks. It has been such an eye-opener to witness and share in each other's spiritual strengths. If I hadn't been ill, I would have looked outside my circle of loved ones for people that exude spiritual strength, when all along, I have been surrounded by them.

Occasionally, we come across people who possess a spiritual strength that can be truly inspiring. For Doug, one of those persons has been Joel Fleishman, whom Doug met when he was a student at Duke University and Joel was vice chancellor of the school. Doug became Joel's research assistant. He saw how Joel integrated his faith and ethics into his everyday life and the impact he had on people's lives by loving and caring, not preaching. Each day, Joel prayed in the morning, in the afternoon, and at night. Without fail, he recognized the holy days of his religion. On the Sabbath, he took time to meditate and read religious writings, and even more time to pray. He did not wear his religion on his sleeve, yet spoke frankly about God, faith, ethics, and higher responsibilities. Doug says that during his college years he learned more about spirituality from Joel than from any other person.

➤ Spending time with spiritual people can reinforce your faith and dedication to your highest priorities, and can allow you to explore meaningful spiritual issues that may otherwise go ignored.

❏ Resolve issues that have come between you and others in your life.

I believe my spirit will have to address the hurt I have caused other spirits, whether in this lifetime or in heaven. Several books by people who had near-death experiences recount that during the process of dying, the authors had to experience the pain they had caused other people. Whether we each will face this pain or not, it is a traumatic idea to think that our spirits would feel so unsettled by the pain we had inflicted on others. Among those who recounted these stories, some said they had hurt people without knowing it. My approach is to clean up things now.

➤ Contact people whom you have hurt in some way or about whom you feel remorse. Ask for their forgiveness. Bring issues that have come between you out in the open. Use forethought, diplomacy, and love.

❏ Host a dinner party with friends to talk about spiritual issues.

Doug and I have enjoyed spending evenings with friends talking about spiritual issues. Our conversations were thought-provoking and gave us a chance to become closer to our friends on a spiritual level.

➤ Consider arranging for a few friends to get together to talk about spiritual issues. One word of caution, however: Do not focus on religion or religious dogma. People tend to have strong opinions on religion, and the conversation may get heated or unpleasant. We recommend sticking to spiritual issues, such as:

- How does one talk to God?
- What tricks can one use to quiet the mind for meditation and prayer?
- Is there life after death?
- If there is life after death, what might it be like?
- What are one's thoughts on dying?
- After the death of a relative or friend, does one's relationship with God change?

❏ Read inspiring books (or listen to inspiring books on tape).

After reading inspirational books or listening to tapes, I feel a stronger connection to my spiritual core and to the people around me. In particular, when I've faced difficult issues or have felt sad or low, reading spiritual books helped me create a connection to the world around me. Everything became vivid and more precious. Spiritual books or tapes have often put me in a frame of mind in which it was easier to see God's work in my life.

➤ Reading spiritual materials can challenge your beliefs, whether you agree or disagree with what is written. Thinking about and questioning your beliefs present an opportunity to deepen your spirituality and avoid the stagnation that can come from complacence.

❏ Rejoice in your trials.

I have often been asked the question, "Why do bad things happen to good people?" Behind the question, I think, is the temptation to believe that life should be fair. Our loved ones shouldn't get sick or face misfortune. Some shouldn't have easy lives while others struggle just to get by.

I don't agree with this line of thinking. Instead, I am thankful for the last four years. Without my illness, I would not have experienced so much emotional and spiritual growth. I would have continued to live my easy life, coasting along, and would have missed out on all there was to learn by facing up to the challenge. We live for the growth of the soul. By handling the trials and tribulations that come our way, we can grow and become closer to God. Without trials, there would be no purpose for an earthly existence. Rather, life would be utopia, and we would be living in heaven. But we are not in heaven, and while on earth, our souls can grow closer to God. I feel blessed because I have had this chance to become closer to God. Unless I could accomplish the same growth without having cancer, I would not trade these last years for anything.

Doug's trials have been different from mine, yet he too has grown over the last few years. Doug has taken strength from Romans 5:1–6, which reads: "More than that, rejoice in our sufferings, knowing that suffering produces endurance, and endurance produces character, and character produces hope, and hope does not disappoint us, because God's love has been poured into our hearts through the Holy Spirit which has been given to us." Over the last four years, as Doug has endured with me the trials of having cancer, his response has been very much in keeping with this scripture. At first, he suffered with me as I went through the grueling treatments, and our lives remained in perpetual crisis mode. Then he built up his endurance and found himself able to handle more than he would have thought possible. With endurance came character development as he saw his view of the world shift and felt himself get closer to God. Hope emerged when he realized he had God by his side, supporting each step. With hope, he could receive God's love.

❏ Consider attending a religious service.

The day after Doug's parents moved to Dallas, his mother was admitted to the hospital for what turned out to be a two-month stay. Sadly, she spent eight of the next eleven months there, and Doug's father had to manage her care in a city where he knew no one other than Doug, me, and my parents. What gave Doug's dad some relief was attending a local church. Not only did he find spiritual sustenance in the weekly services, but within a matter of weeks of his arrival, the congregation adopted Doug's dad into the church family. New friends brought him food, visited the hospital room, prayed for his wife's recovery, asked him out for meals, and invited him to join the choir and participate in other activities. The dynamic church community gave him a level of spiritual and social support that carried him through a very difficult time and is a mainstay of his life to this day.

> ➤ If you so choose, attending religious services can offer fellowship, education, and prayer support, and can create a foundation for your children's spiritual development.

❏ **Live your life out of your sense of purpose.**

I realized if I was a prism through which God's light and love flowed, my obligation was to keep that prism as clean as possible. I was to do my best to live my life according to His standards of goodness and allow His love to flow through me to others. Each morning, as I woke up and lay in bed, I found myself thinking, I have another day on earth, another chance to fulfill my purpose. That way, as I went through my busy day, my purpose did not waver, but guided my decisions and allocation of time. For example, when friends interrupt my day because they need help in handling a personal crisis, I try to remember that my purpose in life includes being there for others in their time of need. Instead of listening with only one ear or rushing off to deal with more pressing matters, I now give my friends and family members my full attention. By focusing on what I can do for them, we become much more connected.

> ➤ Each morning, whether you are healthy or ill, consider that you have another day to live your life and can have an impact on the people around you. Think about how you can integrate into your daily life what's important to you, and how you might let your own purpose on earth shine through. Like me, you might find your mind calming down while you actually enjoy and accomplish more each

day. As you discover your purpose in the world, allow your convictions to govern your actions every day.

IF YOU ARE LIVING WITH A SERIOUS ILLNESS

❏ Invite spiritual people to pray with you.

Spiritual people have offered to pray with me, and I have said yes to every opportunity. For this, though, it was important first to spend time with each person to get a feeling for his or her relationship with God. If the person spoke directly to God and let His love flow through, I would get strength from our prayer together. If, however, he or she was trying to find an individual connection and was more like a cheerleader for God, I would find the experience draining or distracting. With the truly spiritual people, I found our time praying together enormously uplifting. I have invited "prayer warriors" (my nickname for especially spiritual people, including our minister) to help me through my recurring spiritual crises. During three times when my body was suffering, my spirit felt too weak to find strength in God by myself.

Typically, a spiritual friend or minister would come over and ask what was occurring for me spiritually and physically and ask what I needed praying for. By answering these questions, I would pinpoint my weaknesses, concerns, or anxieties that were keeping my spirit from being lifted by God. The prayer warrior would invariably have the words from God to lift me out of it. One spiritual friend in particular received visions on my behalf at a time when she did not know what was occurring in my life. When she told me about what she had heard in her visions, I realized they were a direct answer to my silent concerns and conversations with God. That she had no way of knowing what was going through my head made me feel certain her messages came straight from God. As with so many of my spiritual friends,

I am indebted to this woman because she gives of her time and energy every week without asking anything in return.

> ➤ If you are looking for strength and spiritual sustenance, I recommend inviting spiritual people to pray with you. If you do not know someone to ask, call a hospice, church, synagogue, or mosque and ask for their recommendations.

❏ **Place yourself on as many prayer lists as you can.**

Throughout my battle with cancer, I have been convinced that prayer has kept me alive. When my family and friends prayed for me, I have come through life-threatening situations. This has happened repeatedly, sometimes immediately following a particularly powerful meeting of a prayer group or a concentrated effort by my spiritual friends and family members. So I have learned to boldly encourage family and friends to include me on their prayer lists at their places of worship, in their Bible study classes, or even on special occasions. In several instances, without my prompting, my cousin has sent a card to all my friends and family members, asking everyone to pray on a certain day at a particular time. These "global" prayer sessions gave me an immense feeling of God's love and strength.

> ➤ The power of prayer has been extensively documented. Researchers have conducted tests on microbes in petri dishes, small animals, and humans; they have scientifically demonstrated that prayer influences the activities of organisms. For humans in particular, prayer has been shown to dramatically improve a person's healing from illness or surgery. The book *Healing Words*, by Larry Dossey, M.D., includes the accumulated scientific data on this subject.

❏ **Create a prayer group.**

A year ago, shortly after my battle with cancer took a turn for the worse, several special friends from high school decided to start a prayer group for me. It was a bold move because they were all from different religious backgrounds and had never even talked about spiritual issues together. At first, my friends had no idea how to go about organizing the group. What does one do at a prayer group? They decided to invite a minister to lead the first session and help them set up guidelines. The minister told them they could talk about the person they were praying for; they could share quiet time for prayer together; they could read scripture; or they could follow any number of other formats for the gatherings.

The prayer sessions have evolved over the last year, but several fixtures have remained. They start each session with an update on my health and any specific prayer requests by participants. Participants also discuss with the group (if something important has occurred for them spiritually) or they talk about the role of spirituality in their lives. Each prayer group concludes with a circle of prayer. Everyone stands and holds hands together, with their eyes closed and heads bowed. Each person says a prayer out loud, then squeezes the hand of the next person to let that person know it's his or her turn. If someone does not want to pray aloud, he or she simply lets the next person know it's his or her turn by squeezing hands. No refreshments are served, so the gatherings do not become social occasions; they remain spiritual. Doug and I participated in the prayer group once and were incredibly moved by the feelings and emotions.

Amazingly, this group has met almost weekly for a year and has sometimes convened on last-minute notice when I have faced a sudden crisis. For this, we are immensely grateful. Their relationships with each other have reached a depth that they doubt would ever have happened without these intimate spiritual connections. The prayer group has become such an important part of their lives that several participants plan always to have a group. Recently, they have decided to share ideas for developing spirituality in their children.

❏ **Create your own Sabbath service if you cannot attend religious services.**

When I am feeling ill, Doug, Peyton, and I try to set aside half a day to create our own Sabbath service. We start the morning by reading from Peyton's children's Bible. (Simplified children's versions of religious texts are available for most religions.) Doug and I have found that the stories in the children's Bible are especially vivid, memorable, and fun to share together. Often the stories we talk about inspire us during the week and help guide us in our daily choices. We have also found these conversations to be an opportune time to talk about life after death in the context of heaven and a relationship with God.

At other times, a friend has created a service for me in my home.

➤ I recommend creating your own Sabbath service for you, your family, and friends if you cannot attend your own religious services. Our family has come to love this time together.

❏ **Create an environment that is conducive to spirituality.**

In my bedroom, where I spend a great deal of time, I have tried to create an environment that is conducive to spirituality. My spiritual readings lie within arm's reach. In several spots in the room, I have spiritual icons that I can use as focal points when I am not feeling well. Nearby, I keep a small tape player with scripture on tape. Sometimes when I wake up at night, feeling weak and anxious, I will listen to one of these tapes, using earphones so as not to disturb Doug. Listening to the positive affirmations calms me down, and I often fall back to sleep with them playing in my ears.

When Doug's mother was in the hospital for several months, his father made a concerted effort to create a spiritual ambiance in her room. He played spiritual tapes, periodically read scripture to her, and arranged for the hospital pastor to visit regularly. His mother was uplifted by these efforts. In the tranquillity that his Dad helped create, Doug's mother reached her own spiritual peace before her death.

❏ Allow for divine intervention to ease your passing.

Before Doug's mother died, she asked for God's strength, peace and healing. Her leg had recently been amputated and she was fighting a very painful infection. Although in the end she was not physically healed, she felt that God gave her peace and strength. During her final days, Doug saw in her a glow he had never seen before. Nurses, doctors, and pastors all commented on the tranquillity that she projected, which was in such contrast to her physical torment. Knowing that his mother died in peace, having been fully prepared spiritually for her death, was a great comfort to Doug, his dad, and his brother.

For a long time, the saying, "You are born alone and you die alone" bothered me. I certainly did not want to face the prospect of being so alone in death. I feel very differently now that I have my own relationship with God. I know now that God was present when I was born and will be present when I die. I believe God will bring me peace at my death, as He did during my near-death experience. When I nearly died, I learned from God that death could be beautiful if I reached out to Him. He would help me through the transition, if I chose to include him. Ultimately, the choice was mine.

CHAPTER SUMMARY

- ❏ Decide if you believe in a higher being.
- ❏ Decide whether you believe in a separation of body and spirit.
- ❏ Establish your own personal relationship with God.
- ❏ Write down any questions or fears you have about God.
- ❏ Learn and take time to meditate.
- ❏ Pray.
- ❏ If you are married, say nightly prayers aloud with your partner.

❒ Pray with your children.
❒ Be patient with your spiritual development.
❒ Look for God's work in your life.
❒ Read your religion's holy works.
❒ Learn about the religions of the world.
❒ Find a spiritual advisor or mentor.
❒ Allocate time to spend with people who exude spiritual strength.
❒ Resolve issues that have come between you and others in your life.
❒ Host a dinner party with friends to talk about spiritual issues.
❒ Read inspiring books (or listen to inspiring books on tape).
❒ Rejoice in your trials.
❒ Consider allocating a day each week for spiritual reflection.
❒ Live your life out of your sense of purpose.

If You Are Living with a Serious Illness
❒ Invite spiritual people to pray with you.
❒ Place yourself on as many prayer lists as you can.
❒ Create a prayer group.
❒ Create your own Sabbath service if you cannot attend religious services.
❒ Create an environment that is conducive to spirituality.
❒ Allow for divine intervention to ease your passing.

8

EXPECT TO LIVE: LIVING WITH ABUNDANCE AND LOVE

Who would have thought that by embracing my mortality, I would feel so alive? What a surprise it was to find that looking at my life with the end in mind—and in so doing, identifying my purpose and priorities—would give me the perspective I needed to live my life fully . . . and not just go through the motions.

Five years ago, if anyone had asked me if I expected to live, I would have thought the question silly. Of course I expected to live, what was the alternative? Now I am well aware of the alternative. The question for all of us is, what are we doing between now and when we die? Are we living life with a sense of meaning and purpose, feeling alive in the moment and blessed by the what we have and are able to experience each day? Before I got cancer, Doug and I certainly weren't. We worked hard, loved our family and friends, yet generally felt caught up in the whirlwind of our lives. We functioned at the whim of the greatest demands on our time. Then, with acceptance of our mortality, a whole new understanding of "expect to live" dawned on us. We could choose to live our lives out of a sense of purpose, or we could allow our priorities to be dictated by what others thought was important. This is not to say that the daily challenge of jug-gling our various responsibilities disappeared. It didn't. The dif-ference was we had a new filtering mechanism for deciding what to take on each day. Realizing we were on the right path, and knew where we were headed, as individuals and as a couple, felt exciting and also peaceful. "Expect to live" meant expect to live fully and wholeheartedly.

Living with "the end in mind" had ramifications beyond my individual sense of purpose in the world. Doug and I found our-selves looking at our marriage, our parenting, and his career with the longer view in mind. We thought about our lives in terms of where we wanted to end up, rather than just in terms of what needed to be done tomorrow or the next day. We visu-alized the hoped-for destination and then worked backwards.

Now that you have completed your checklist, you have the remainder of your life to live with reduced stress, to concentrate on love, laughter, and living. You have completed your "have-tos" with the checklists; now do your "want-tos." This chapter looks at your goals vis-à-vis living with the end in mind, and at ways of living life fully, surrounded by love and laughter. With the completion of the checklist, we hope you experience peace and that your life will be filled with new discoveries.

❏ Identify your life goals as an individual.

A friend came to me recently saying he felt exhausted and unfulfilled, despite having a happy family and a good career. His life was careening along, and he wasn't enjoying it. We decided to look at his priorities. We wrote down everything that was important to him, including things he did now and things he wanted to do. Next, we wrote down how he allotted his time. What a contrast between his priorities and his schedule! On paper, it was completely understandable why he felt his life was off track. We set about creating realistic changes to his schedule so that he could incorporate more of his life goals and priorities into his daily existence.

➤ I recommend allocating an evening, a half day, or even a weekend to spending time with your thoughts. With a pencil and a pad of paper in hand, think about your life coming to an end and work backwards. Look back at your remaining life and ask yourself:

- How do I want my life to unfold?
- What do I hope to accomplish?
- What relationships do I want to have?
- What feelings do I want to experience?
- What mark do I want to leave on this earth?

I suggest heeding three guidelines for this exercise: (1) Have fun. Thinking about what makes you feel happy and fulfilled should be enjoyable. Use this opportunity to play with new ideas, try on old ones, see what fits best for you. Give yourself time to think about your life in ways you never have before, knowing that only you can determine if you are living a life you are proud of. (2) Try not to think in terms of what your colleagues, parents, or spouse might expect of you. Instead, think about what would make you feel at peace with yourself and your life, were it to come to an end. By this, I do not mean ignore the consequences of your choices or your impact on other souls. Rather, I recommend a true and thorough evaluation of your life direction, knowing that you are seeking peace of mind with your eventual death (This assumes, of course, that peace of mind would be difficult to find if you indiscriminately and selfishly hurt others).

I found it difficult to separate the "social" mirror from my expectations of myself. However, given time and contemplation (and the advantage of having had a near-death experience), from the assumptions and expectations around me, I eventually distinguished who I was and who I wanted to be.

(3) The third guideline is to not dwell on what life has been up to now. Look to the future, starting in this exact moment in time. The possibility to change one's life or heal and start new relationships exists in the moment. It is your choice. You can choose your attitude, coping mechanism, and goals for your life.

❏ **Identify your life goals for your career.**

Before I got cancer, I was a career-driven person, with my sense of self-worth largely tied to my professional accomplishments. But then, as I lay on the brink of death in the hospital room, not a single thought about my ten-year career as a venture capitalist went through my head. No memory of my work came to me. It was shocking and disheartening to realize that my career, which at the time had been so stimulating and exciting, meant so little to me in the end, particularly given how much time and energy I had devoted to it. Instead, my thoughts, judgments, and feelings of peace centered on my relationships with other souls and with God. I evaluated life in terms of how I treated the people with whom I had come in contact, in particular my family and friends. I came away from the near-death experience knowing that it did not matter what I did professionally, but **how** I did it. I could become a painter, a janitor, a corporate executive; it did not matter in the end. Did I bring God's love to the people around me?

To be clear, I did not come away from this experience thinking we should all stop working or change our careers. Not only do we need to earn a living, but as individuals, we thrive on doing work that we are proud of. Even more importantly, in the workplace, we can have a tremendous impact on other people and their financial, emotional, physical, and even spiritual well-being. We all know the power that one person's decisions and commitments can have on hundreds or thousands of people. A career is important, but for reasons that go far beyond financial rewards and professional accomplishments.

➤ The question to ask yourself is, are you making career choices with the end in mind? Each day, are you going about your work knowing that you have an effect on the souls around you and can choose to have a positive or negative impact on them?

➤ Set your career goals as measured by your own personal definition of professional success, rather than by goals as measured by your colleagues.

❏ **Identify your life goals as a spouse and as a couple.**

Doug and I would not have traded the last four years for the world. The trials of the cancer have been small in comparison to the enormous growth we have experienced as individuals and as a couple. The greatest breakthrough came in our communication with each other. When the cancer first hit, we ignored the need to talk about what was happening—until we both were ready to explode with pent-up stress and emotions. Then, we became more deliberate about talking together and sharing our fears, worries, hopes, and dreams. What a discovery! Knowing we could talk to each other about anything and could face any challenge together was an incredible eye-opener. That's what marriage was all about. We could go through whatever trials came our way if we relied on each other and talked our way through.

Not only that, but we could look ahead, with the end in mind, and define how we wanted our marriage to unfold, and what we needed to do now to make it easier on each other if either of us should pass away.

Doug and I have borrowed a New Year's Eve tradition from my parents. On a typical New Year's Eve, we lit a fire, put Peyton to bed, and settled into the living room to talk about our dreams and goals for ourselves and as a couple. With two pads of paper and pens, we each wrote down one-year and five-year goals for ourselves and for us as a couple. Then, after we got our ideas down on paper, we read each other our lists and talked about them. The idea wasn't to come up with long, tedious to-do lists, but to have some fun with all areas of our lives. Within the categories of physical, mental, emotional and spiritual, we wrote goals for work, family, friends, culture, travel, exercise, spirituality, and other areas as they came to us. We looked out to the future and imagined interesting and exciting things to do and accomplish, either together or separately. It was during one of these conversations that we came up with the idea of traveling to Africa. Until our "goals-and-dreams" conversation, we didn't realize we each had wanted to visit Africa, but had discounted the idea because it was too expensive and time consuming. Once we wrapped our minds around the trip, we started planning and saving. We went to Africa four years ago and had the time of our lives.

During these goal-setting conversations, we also realized something about our marriage: our relationship with each other came first. Everything else was second, including our relationship with Peyton. When I was growing up, my parents told me that their love for each other came before their love for me and my siblings. To some people, this might sound unloving, but I did not see it that way. Knowing they were taking care of each other and looking after their relationship gave me a great sense of security. It was important for Doug and me to have a strong marriage so that Peyton would have that same sense of love and security as well as a good example for her future marriage. Doug and I take two weeks of vacation every year—one week as a couple and another as a family. I believe that parents who always put their children's needs ahead of their spouse's, to the point that they won't take vacations without their children, can potentially destabilize the family. Everything in a family revolves around that love and solidity of the parents' relationships with each other.

➤ Write down fun and exciting goals for yourself (there's no need to wait until New Year's Eve). Why not create a plan for your marriage? We create plans for other areas of life—business plans, financial plans, or even household management plans—but don't give our own hopes and dreams the same attention. Talk to each other about your hopes and dreams for your marriage. Look out to the future and imagine your life together—the circumstances of your life, how you will interact, what you will have done together, why you will continue to love each other so much.

➤ One of the great things about sharing this exercise with someone you care about is that you get to learn what is most important to him or her. So often, we get caught up in the day-to-day happenings of our lives that we forget the big picture. Sharing goals and dreams offers a reminder that what we are doing today is a stepping stone to where we are going tomorrow.

➤ As a couple, if there are issues that have gone unspoken or have come between you, clean the slate. Set aside time to talk, just the two of you, and let one person talk uninterrupted while the other takes notes and listens. Then, switch and let the other person talk uninterrupted. Know that your goal is to listen and really hear what is on the other person's mind. Wait until everything is said before trying to fix any problems or offer solutions. Also know that there may not be easy solutions to every issue raised. Some things might take time to figure out. Go through the list of issues raised and choose which ones to work on first. The goal is to address any issues together rather than separately.

❏ **Feed your soul.**

Take time for activities that nourish and enliven your soul. For each person, these activities are different. Among the possibilities are listening to or playing favorite pieces of music, reading (or being read) poetry or inspiring passages, enjoying a bouquet of flowers, lighting a fire in the fireplace, planning a special occasion, strolling under the trees, laughing with your loved ones, getting a massage, praying. The list of possibilities goes on and on. Find what gratifies your soul, and take time to enjoy the activity thoroughly. Breathe deeply and feel the positive energy flow through you.

❏ **Laugh and play.**

When I was in the hospital bubble room, Doug and our coauthor Emily organized a funniest card contest. Here I was fighting for my life, and they came up with the perfect release. Everyone in my life was so frightened about my prognosis that they loved having an excuse to reach out to me with love and humor. Friends and relatives from all over the country sent hundreds of funny cards. When I recovered, Doug and I had a hilarious time reading all the entries. We awarded a prize to the person whose card made us laugh the hardest, and we sent copies of the top contenders to everyone who had entered our contest.

Looking back on our lives, Doug and I especially relish the times when we have played hard. Whether it was rafting down the Zambezi River, having full-blown water fights in our first house, getting up at daybreak to go bass fishing, going all out with decorations and props for Peyton's Pocahontas birthday party, or playing the annual Kramp Turkey Bowl football game on Thanksgiving Day when the field was one big mud puddle—spirited playing has given spice to our lives. Expecting to live includes playing hard when we have the time and the energy to do so.

➤ Laughing is such an incredible pleasure, and yet we get so busy, it can be hard to find time to laugh and play with our families, friends, and co-workers. I suggest scheduling playtime just as you would a business meeting or dental appointment. Share a special meal with people you don't get to see often enough. See a funny movie. Play board games or other group activities that get people laughing. Think of your own ways to have special fun times with people you love.

❏ **Involve other people in your life.**

Innumerable research studies have demonstrated that lonely people have shorter life expectancies than people with loved ones in their lives. Love and companionship boost the immune system; life is richer and more meaningful when it is shared with other people. The good news about the research coming out is, you do not have to up and get married or move in with somebody. One study, conducted at Stanford University, showed that women with metastatic breast cancer who participated in a weekly support group lived twice as long as women who did not have a support group. After five years, the only women still alive were those who were a part of the support group. Many of the support-group participants expressed initial reservations about interacting with people they did not know, but after spending months in the program, said they wouldn't give up the camaraderie and chance to share themselves with other people.

In another study, conducted by the University of Texas Medical School, researchers found that men and women who had elective open-heart surgery were four times more likely to live six months after surgery if they participated in organized social groups (clubs, church, synagogue, civic activities) than if they did not. These same people were three times more likely to live if they drew comfort and strength from their religious or spiritual faith.

➤ If you are living a lonely existence, I highly recommend finding ways to involve other people in your life. The trick is having some fun thinking about the options. Make a game of thinking of how many ideas you can come up with. Then, try out the top three or four on your list. You'll be amazed at how much fun you can have, and how much easier it is to reach out to people than you might think. Even if you are bedridden or disabled, there are ways to involve other people in your life. Here are some things to think about:

- Join a local church, synagogue, or temple and participate in its programs. If you cannot get out, ask if someone from the organization can visit you at your home.
- Organize a book club (that can meet at your house if
  you have difficulty getting out). Organize a family
  reunion or write a family newsletter (which would give
  you a reason to stay in regular touch with parents, siblings, and relatives).
- Call or write family members or friends with whom you
  have lost touch. Invite them back into your life.
- Visit a local nursing home.
- Take a class in yoga and meditation.
- Volunteer your time at an after-school program for kids
  at risk.
- If you like to travel, join a group tour to a favorite destination.
- If you are athletic, join a runners club, a tennis league,
  or sign up for a rafting trip.
- Try out a new activity or interest that you've always
  wanted to try.

❑ **Give to others.**

Albert Einstein said:

*Strange is our situation here upon earth. Each of us comes for a
short visit, not knowing why, yet sometimes seeming to divine a
purpose. From the standpoint of daily life, however there is one
thing we do know: That we are here for the sake of others . . . for
the countless unknown souls with whose fate we are connected by
a bond of sympathy. Many times a day, I realize how much my
outer and inner life is built upon the labors of people, both living
and dead, and how earnestly I must exert myself to give in
return as much as I have received.*

Doug and I feel we have been given so much. We are not
referring to money or other material goods, but love, grace,

family, friends, and the prayers of others. Our list of blessings goes on and on. It has been up to us to make time and reach out to others who are less fortunate. It has not always been easy to do so, but whenever we have, it was incomparably refreshing to step outside our narrow world. Giving to others provides a chance to open up the airways and inhale the exhilarating sensation of touching other people in ways that are important to them.

❏ Minimize chitchat.

One surprising aspect of having cancer is that I have had the most amazing conversations with people, not just people I know well, but all sorts who have crossed my path for the briefest of moments. Before getting cancer, I never would have realized how much others have to say and contribute to my understanding of the world, or how much wisdom there is around me. People want to talk about their hopes and dreams and personal challenges, but they are rarely asked. We feel constrained by the inconsequential chitchat that tends to dictate how we communicate with one another. I recommend slowing down and listening to the people around you. Imagine that each person you come in contact with is put on this earth to teach you something. You will be amazed by what happens when you eliminate chitchat.

❏ Find reasons to celebrate.

Celebrations remind us in large and small ways how wonderful it is to be alive. Without them, life would be very dull indeed. Celebrations can come with everyday activities or with big festivities around major occasions. Last year, Doug and I celebrated our tenth wedding anniversary with a big party at the same locale where we had had our wedding reception. We made the party special; with the help of my brother, Michael, and a friend I composed a song for Doug that a professional musician played at the party, and Doug created a video from the photographs we had of ourselves with our friends who were there at the party (and had been with us when we were married ten years before).

❏ **Be sensitive to the effects of stress on your body.**

It is common knowledge that we live in a stressful world. And that stress is bad for one's health. Whether you are healthy or ill, it is important to find ways to release the stress you are under. For Doug, he needs exercise. If he doesn't work out, he becomes tightly wound. For me, when I am feel under a great deal of stress, I need to hide out from the world for a short while. I find writing in my journal can be very therapeutic and also find rejuvenation in prayer, meditation, reading, and spiritual music, all of which work to shut off the negative chatter going on in my head.

❏ **Listen to spiritually uplifting music.**

Listening to uplifting music is a gift to your spirit. If I am feeling down or alone, music can immediately shift my mind-set from the negative to the positive. When inspiring music is playing, I find myself noticing the beauty around me and feeling grateful for all that I have. Music can provide an excellent transition from a busy day to quieting the mind for meditation or prayer.

> ➤ Try listening to a piece of music without doing anything else. If you close your eyes while the music is playing, you might find you actually hear the music better. Try out different music that has been written for the glory of God, whether Gregorian chants, gospel music, hymns, or other spirituals.

❏ **Eat healthy foods, which give clarity of mind and are less taxing on your body.**

Organic foods might be a bit more expensive, but Doug and I decided they're worth the expense. One never knows the long-term effects of pesticides and growth hormones on our bodies. Researchers still don't know why the rates of some forms of cancer keep rising, so we would just as soon play it safe. The foods that can have the highest concentrations of pesticides or growth hormones are meats, dairy products, fruit juices, and jams and jellies. Our view is, we'll buy organic foods for our home, knowing that we will get plenty of processed foods in restaurants and at friends' homes. Without obsessing about the foods we eat, we try to balance good foods with the processed ones. Otherwise, our view is, if God created the food, we can eat it in moderation (unless there is a medical reason not to). Other thoughts on diet and health are to

- Avoid white sugar and artificial sweeteners
- Lower alcohol intake
- Avoid fatty processed foods
- Eliminate tobacco
- Visit a health food store and try its offerings
- Read articles on health and nutrition
- Seek moderation in your diet (no extremes)

❏ **Get plenty of sleep.**

I don't function well when I am sleep deprived. I don't think as clearly, and I'm not as happy or as loving to my family and friends as I am when I get enough sleep. I know this about myself, but still, it is difficult to get eight hours of sleep each night. There are so many demands on my time. It is easier to set my alarm clock a little early or stay up too late to get everything done. Across America, sleep deprivation is a widespread problem, with all sorts of studies being conducted and news articles being written on its impact.

For myself, getting enough sleep is partly a matter of discipline. I have to force myself to keep to a schedule and not let the demands of the day intrude on my need for rest. This can be especially hard if I am enjoying a special evening with friends or am in the middle of an important project, but I'm getting better at listening to my body and extricating myself from whatever is keeping me from getting enough rest. During the times when I cannot fall asleep, I find it helpful just to rest quietly, relaxing

my mind and body. At these times, I find it particularly important not to get upset at the insomnia because then I'll feel only
more tired the next day.

❏ Appreciate nature.

When Doug was young, his grandmother used to teach him
about the animals, insects, flowers and trees that were on his
grandparents' farm. Her love and appreciation for the simple
beauties in nature rubbed off on him early on. Similarly, I have
always loved the outdoors. When our lives accelerate to the
point that we are well past our own speed limits, it is difficult to
take notice of the beauty around us. In contrast, it is such a pleasure to notice ladybugs on our picture window when our lives
are in balance and at peace.

❏ Listen for the birds.

Every morning when you wake up, listen for the birds. They
are a daily reminder that we have another day on earth, another
opportunity to touch a soul with God's love.

IF YOU ARE LIVING WITH A SERIOUS ILLNESS

❏ Write down fun and exciting goals for yourself.

Since learning that my cancer was terminal, I have created
goals for myself to keep me focused on the future. As I mentioned earlier in this book, my first goal was to live to see my
daughter's fifth birthday. I knew that by the time a child turned
five, her basic personality was formed, and I wanted to be there
for this important first phase of Peyton's life. After celebrating
her fifth birthday, I broke down and cried because it had been
such an important occasion to me and I was so grateful to be
there. My subsequent goals have been shorter term—living to
celebrate my tenth anniversary, seeing our *20/20* and *Oprah*

broadcasts, writing this book. Each one has given purpose to my day and something to look forward to as I go through treatments and the ups and downs of my prognosis.

➤ Write new achievable goals for yourself. These goals should have one- or two-month time frames and can include trips; books to read, write, or have read to you; and people to talk to. After attaining a goal, set a new one. At no point should you be without goals in mind. Make the goals fun and joyous. Even if you are bedridden, you can have wonderful experiences.

❏ **Add fun and humor to your life.**

Emily's mother-in-law had cancer and let her three sons and Emily organize a birthday party for her. People traveled from all over to join the party, share funny anecdotes, and tell her how much they loved her. She did not have to do anything in the planning—just show up and enjoy the celebration of her life. It was a magical party that touched everyone who came.

➤ Even if you are bedridden, there are ways to add fun and humor to your life and give you a fresh opportunity to share laughter with friends and family.

❏ **Cherish your body.**

There have been times that my body has felt like the enemy, letting me down and leaving me utterly exhausted. To counteract this, I found that nourishing my body in small ways improved my frame of mind enormously. Whether it was from being touched or massaged, taking baths, eating well, or getting outside in the sunshine, these small efforts made me feel more human and whole.

➤ Know what makes your body feel more physically strong and whole, and ask your family, friends, and caregivers to provide you with what you need. Following are some of the ways I have tried to cherish and reconnect with my body:

1. **Be touched.** I have talked with a lot of people about the need to be touched when you are feeling ill. They all agree that it's very important. When people are sick, they can go a long time without feeling the loving touch of another person, which can be terribly isolating. There have been times when I was lying in bed, either in a hospital or at home, that I longed for hugs from my husband, my daughter or my parents. Of course, when I was feeling particularly ill, visitors to my bedside did not think to hug me or hold my hand for fear of upsetting my fragile health. I would have to ask or hope that people would reach out to me on their own. There were times when Doug felt as though I were hidden behind a medical fortress—an almost impenetrable armor of oxygen tubes, IVs, and other health care paraphernalia. It took a concerted effort on his part to get past these obstacles and touch me.

   Feeling the warmth and strength of a loved one gave me great comfort. I have felt a jolt of energy from touching someone I cared about. I also have enjoyed gentle massage. Sometimes a family member has massaged my feet or hands, or I have engaged a masseuse to give me reflexology or a mild full body massage.

   After the leg of Doug's mother was amputated, she was immobilized and in pain. To comfort her, Doug's Dad rubbed her back, arms and leg. At night, he rubbed her neck and shoulders to put her asleep. She never had to comment on the massage, just relax into his sensitive touch. Her facial expression and body language were indications of the comfort she received.

➤ If you are a caregiver, make a conscious effort to touch the person you are supporting. If you feel uncertain, ask if the person would like you to hold his or her hand, massage their temples or feet, or just hug them.

2. **Take baths**. I have come to love baths. I take baths in the evening after Peyton has gone to bed and I am ready to turn in for the night. I fill the bath with hot water and just soak. I find it easy to let my mind wander during a bath. Meditation comes naturally once I have let the warm water and steam relax me. Sometimes, if I have had a particularly difficult day, I play inspiring tapes on the tape recorder, which I keep in the bathroom for that purpose.

3. **Get outside into the sunshine.** When I'm not feeling well, I have had to spend days on end in the house or the hospital without feeling the sun on my face or a breeze in my hair. As a remedy, when the weather has been nice, Doug occasionally has moved an easy chair outside so I could catch a few minutes of sunshine. If I was feeling particularly weak, he carried me to the chair and wrapped me in a blanket to ward off a chill. The sun has life-giving properties; you can feel the energy seep through your body as its rays warm your face. These moments in the sun were incredibly refreshing and rejuvenating.

❏ **Read healing and uplifting books.**

I have found there are many good books that look at physical and spiritual healing in ways that are uplifting. If you are unable to go to the library or bookstore, ask someone to go for you and bring back a list of titles of books that look promising. Another option is to ask someone to go on-line to a bookseller on the Internet, such as www.amazon.com, and print the summaries of books on healing, spirituality, and wellness. With that information in hand, you can select the books you would like to order through the Internet. The on-line bookseller will deliver the books to your address after you pay with a credit card for your purchase.

❏ Take care of your appearance.

People I have talked to who are managing a serious illness agree that taking care of your appearance can raise your spirits. For me, when I wear nice-looking, comfortable clothes and am well put together, I feel better about myself. On the days when I wear the same old clothes, don't bother with makeup or getting cleaned up, I feel tired and more sickly.

❏ Turn your pain over to God.

If you experience intense pain, turn this pain, as an offering, over to God and seek peace in the knowledge that your spiritual body will leave this painful physical body and ultimately unite with the Lord. Know that He may not take you with this illness, but you may go on to live for years and years of wholeness.

CHAPTER SUMMARY

❐ Identify your life goals as an individual.
❐ Identify your life goals for your career.
❐ Identify your life goals as a spouse and as a couple.
❐ Feed your soul.
❐ Laugh and play.
❐ Involve other people in your life.
❐ Give to others.
❐ Minimize chitchat.
❐ Find reasons to celebrate.
❐ Be sensitive to the effects of stress on your body.
❐ Listen to spiritually uplifting music.
❐ Eat healthy foods, which give clarity of mind and are less taxing on your body.
❐ Get plenty of sleep.
❐ Appreciate nature.
❐ Listen for the birds.

If You Are Living with a Serious Illness

❐ Write down fun and exciting goals for yourself.
❐ Add fun and humor to your life.
❐ Cherish your body.
❐ Read healing and uplifting books.
❐ Take care of your appearance.
❐ Turn your pain over to God.

Appendix A:
Child Caregiver Interview
Questionnaire
(To be completed by prospective
caregiver)

Some questions to ask a prospective caregiver, either in person or in writing:

1. What do you consider your special talents?
2. What are your greatest strengths?
3. What are your greatest weaknesses?
4. What do you consider your greatest accomplishment?
5. What are your favorite activities for a (age) child?
6. What are your greatest strengths as a child care provider?
7. What are your greatest weaknesses as a child care provider?
8. What age children do you have experience caring for?
9. What is the biggest emergency you have ever had to handle involving a child?
10. What is your preferred discipline for a child?
11. What do you like most about children?
12. What do you like least about children?
13. How do you handle your role in relationship to the parents?
14. Are you willing to abide by the parents' standards?

15. What are the three most important factors you are look-ing for in a caregiver's job?
16. What three factors have you disliked the most in your past jobs?
17. What requests from the family do you like the least?
18. What is the most important response or reward you could expect to receive from an employer?
19. Do you prefer a structured daily routine or a varied and changing daily schedule?
20. What tasks, in addition to basic caregiver's duties, are you capable of and willing to do?
21. Are you willing to travel with a family? What reserva-tions do you have about this?
22. Do you have any outside activities that might conflict with your schedule as a caregiver (i.e., church, school, second jobs, etc.)?
23. How long a commitment are you willing to make?
24. What do you see yourself doing two or three years from now?
25. What are your favorite activities during your free time?
26. Do you have any allergies?
27. Do you smoke?
28. Do you drink?
29. Have you had CPR, first aid, or other medical training?
30. What would you look for in a caregiver if you have your own children?

This next section of the questionnaire is designed to give the parents an understanding of the prospective caregiver's priori-ties. *Ask the caregiver to write down his or her answers to the follow-ing questions:*

1. How would you prioritize the following six aspects of child development? Please explain your rationale.
2. Please give examples of how you would work with a child to develop each of the six aspects of child development.

_____ **Intellectual Development**

_____ **Physical Ability**

_____ **Emotional Development**

_____ **Spiritual Development**

_____ **Discipline**

_____ **Self esteem**

APPENDIX B:
CHECKLIST IN THE EVENT OF DEATH

~⊱❧⊰~

YOUR LOVED ONES WILL NEED TO TAKE THESE ACTIONS IMMEDIATELY UPON YOUR DEATH.

- Prepare the eulogy.
- Select clothing for surviving spouse and children.
- Prepare the home to greet family and friends.
- Sign the necessary papers for burial permit.
- Answer phone calls, letters, and wires of condolence.
- Meet with funeral director and clergy.
- Greet friends and family at service.
- Arrange to meet out-of-town attendees.
- Provide lodging for out-of-town attendees.
- Maintain a list of callers, flower tributes, and donations.
- Order the death certificate.
- Care for infants or minor children.
- Involve the Veteran's Administration in the funeral, if appropriate

MAKE THESE NOTIFICATIONS IMMEDIATELY UPON DEATH.

- Doctor
- Funeral director
- Cemetery and funeral home
- Family members
- Close friends
- Employer of deceased
- Pallbearers

- All insurance agents
- Religious, fraternal and civic organizations
- Local newspapers
- Attorney, accountant and executor of estate
- Social Security office

HANDLE THESE BILLS WHICH WILL BE INCURRED AFTER DEATH.

- Funeral Director
- Clergy
- Florist
- Refreshments
- Clothing
- Doctors
- Nurses
- Hospital and Ambulance
- Medicine and Drugs
- Others: Mortgage or Rent, Taxes, Installment Payments

After the Funeral[6]

Arrange for family members or friends to stay with the surviving spouse as long as they are needed and welcome.

(Note: I recommend assigning an emotionally stable person, who is well known and well liked by the children, to care for them during the entire funeral process. See page 144 for further thoughts on this subject.)

If the deceased lived alone, arrange for the care of pets and maintenance of house and yard. Cancel newspapers and redirect the mail.

Arrange for appropriate medical treatment, and psychological and spiritual counseling for surviving family members. Contact church for names of support groups that can be of help to surviving family members.

Examine contents of the safe-deposit box, any binders or files left by deceased pertaining to financial affairs, insurance, and employee or government benefits. Prepare preliminary inventory of estate.

Contact present or former employers regarding available benefits, including group life insurance, death benefits from retire-

6. First Presbyterian Church, Dallas, Texas, 1993, Exhibit H.

ment plans, major medical coverage for survivors under COBRA, stock options, etc.

Notify Social Security and determine benefits available to survivors. If the deceased was a veteran, notify the Veterans Administration.

File claims for life insurance as soon as death certificates are available. If proceeds are not payable to a trust, confer with the lawyer about placing proceeds in a special account to avoid funds being subject to creditors.

Cancel or amend coverage provided by automobile, homeowners, and other liability policies as well as any supplemental medical or long-term-care insurance, and ask for appropriate refunds.

Cancel credit cards after determining if credit life insurance is in force to cover outstanding balances.

Review checkbooks for at least twelve months to determine if other insurance is in force or if refunds might be available from other sources. Close or restyle checking and savings accounts.

INDEX

ABOUT THE AUTHORS

Erin Tierney Kramp was a venture capitalist for ten years, most recently as a partner with Murchison Capital Partners. Douglas H. Kramp is Executive Vice President/Office of the President of PageMart Wireless. The Kramps live with their daughter, Peyton, in Dallas, Texas.

Emily P. McKhann is a writer and the president of The McKhann Group. She lives in New York City with her husband, Andy Cooper.

If you would like to share with the authors your own checklist items that could be included in future editions of *Living with the End in Mind*, please send your ideas, experiences, and anecdotes to the authors, care of Crown Publishers, Inc., 201 East 50th Street, New York, NY 10022.